Masks

American University Studies

Series VII
Theology and Religion
Vol. 88

PETER LANG
New York • San Francisco • Bern • Baltimore
Frankfurt am Main • Berlin • Wien • Paris

David Blundell

Masks

Anthropology on the Sinhalese Belief System

PETER LANG
New York • San Francisco • Bern • Baltimore
Frankfurt am Main • Berlin • Wien • Paris

Library of Congress Cataloging-in-Publication Data

Blundell, David.
  Masks : anthropology on the Sinhalese belief system / David
Blundell.
    p. cm. — (American university studies. Series VII, Theology
and religion ; vol. 88)
    Includes bibliographical references (p.)
    1. Sri Lanka—Religion—20th century. 2. Sri Lanka—Social life
and customs. 3. Ethnology—Biographical methods. I. Title. II.
Series.
BL2032.S55B58   1994   306.6'095493—dc20   91–36067
ISBN 0-8204-1427-1   CIP
ISSN 0740-0446

Die Deutsche Bibliothek-CIP-Einheitsaufnahme

Blundell, David.
  Masks : anthropology on the Sinhalese belief system / David
Blundell.—New York; Berlin; Bern; Frankfurt/M.; Paris; Wien:
Lang, 1994
    (American university studies: Ser. 7, Theology and Religion; vol. 88)
    ISBN 0-8204-1427-1
NE: American university studies/07

Cover design by George Lallas.

The paper in this book meets the guidelines for permanence and
durability of the Committee on Production Guidelines for Book
Longevity of the Council on Library Resources.

Printed in the United States of America.

Contents

Three: Sinhalese Belief System on Health

Four: Conclusion

References

Text Indices

Cover illustration: Above is a *kibihi mūṇa* (face) which is on guard in the archway (*makara toraṇa*) leading to the sanctum of a temple. The center is represented by a mained lion (*kesara sinha*) which is the legendary ancestor of the Sinhalese.

Figures List

Foreword

AN ANTHROPOLOGY OF SHARING

Jacques Maquet
Professor of Anthropology
University of California, Los Angeles

In the last twenty years or so anthropologists have become increasingly concerned with understanding the culture they study from the point of view of those who live, feel, and think within that culture. Anthropologists want to perceive the culture as the insiders perceive it. And, later, when they present the results of their research they hope that insiders will recognize their own views and feelings and that outsiders also will gain an understanding of the intellectual and affective processes that occur in the insiders' minds.

In his research—and in this book which reflects it—Dr. David Blundell has gone a step further than other sociocultural anthropologists in the quest for understanding and rendering the Sinhalese belief system. His innovative approach is based on sharing the investigative process with those who are usually considered to be objects of the research.

The three parts of the Sinhalese belief system—Theravāda Buddhism, cult of deities, and exorcism—are concretely approached through the life histories of three men. Each plays a key role in one of the three subsystems: headmonk of a village temple, chief official of a shrine, and exorcist. Collecting the story of their lives was a sharing process. David Blundell did not impose, or even propose, his idea of what a biography should include. Each man chose the way he wanted to tell his story. The result may surprise Western readers used to, and thus expecting, highly personal narratives of one's life. The headmonk does not describe, or even mention the personal significance of a celibate's life when as a seventeen-year old youth he decided to embrace it. The reason for this silence is simply that, for a man who has devoted sixty years of his life to eradicating egotism and self-attachment, the fleeting views and feelings of a youthful ego are not worth recording.

Making a biographical film has also been for David Blundell an endeavor to be shared not only with the main character—the headmonk—but also with the village community. Script, shots, sequences were collectively discussed and the final decision was made, like in village meetings, by the most respected elder after all opinions had been presented. After the film had been processed, rushes were screened by the actors and the community.

ix

The montage was again a collective operation. I do not know of any 'ethnographic film' made with such a commitment to the insiders' perspective.

In order to achieve successfully such a delicate sharing, David Blundell had to acquire a deep familiarity with the Sinhalese people and their culture, a deep familiarity which can only be the result of effort, openness, and a long patience. From his first contact with Śrī Lankā, as the guest of a Sinhalese family in Śrī Lankā, to the termination of his third film (on the exorcist), eight years elapsed. During that time, David Blundell made several pre-anthropological sojourns in Śrī Lankā (as a student at Pērādeniya University) and several field research trips. This has made possible the blurring of the distinction between observer and observed.

This book is meant to communicate the Sinhalese understanding of their triadic belief system—the Buddha, the deities, the spirits— through the understanding of a particularly perceptive anthropologist. In this book, the rendering of what he understood, David Blundell again proposes a sharing experience. This time with his readers.

As with the headmonk, the shrine chief, and the exorcist, Blundell does not impose his interpretation. He presents it together with the pieces of evidence on which it is based. The pieces are, of course, facts and observations he has collected. They are also concepts and statements, hypotheses and conclusions he has selected as building blocks or tools in the works of other anthropologists and sociologists. This approach invites readers to participate actively in the construction of their own understanding.

In this regard, this excellent and stimulating book by David Blundell is innovative.

Los Angeles
October 17th, 1987

Preface

This anthropological handbook presents a model for cultural documentation in terms of indigenous values in a religious context. Social factors from the study include aesthetics, life accounts, and belief performances for health. Methodological work followed a plan to utilize recording devices such as the cinecamera to understand various levels of belief in Sinhalese Theravāda Buddhism. This process, useful to *present* the Sinhalese belief system, could be applied to other contexts provided that the researchers have the support and commitment to the tasks required.

Śrī Lankā was always on my mind when I pursued studies in anthropology. It was at the Carrol and Joan Williams' school, Anthropology Film Center, Santa Fe, New Mexico, USA, on a visit to Don and Sue Rundstrom, and Ron Rundstrom and Pat Rosa, when I realized the importance of engaging in research with visual-motion tools for tracing event sequences and life continuities. Following anthropological concepts (especially from Don Rundstrom and Ron Rundstrom) on visually tracking personal and cultural aesthetics for meaning in an enquiry/feedback process, I proceeded to work on *long-term research* under the guidance of A. L. Perera, Punchi Banda Meegaskumbura, and Conrad Ranawake.

Just learning to observe and participate for *action-reading* is not enough. Steps with intention should be followed in suit within cultural matrix. Therefore, a university structure offered an ideal view with a "steering committee" gave comment and literature to put markings on the outcome. In terms of ethnography, I am indebted to L. L. Langness and John G. Kennedy for their psychological life history approach to perceive an individual in culture; and to Douglass Price-Williams for his instruction on symbolic and psychological sensitivity. Following the way of the *individual* in cognitive research, from Gananath Obeyesekere, I obtained experiential orientation on Sinhalese studies of Gananath Obeyesekere. For the process visualizing what I researched and "looking" in a filmic way, much appreciation goes to Richard Hawkins, Michael Moerman, Jorge Preloran, and Jay Ruby. William LaFleur gave much comparative insight in the Buddhist *arc* across East Asia, from participant pilgrimage among Sinhalese and in Japan. Finally, I am most grateful to Jacques Maquet and Hilda Kuper for their rich appreciation of the anthropological ways and means, formalized and alternative, according to the best conceived expression.

For my initial and ongoing South Asian understanding and anthropological theoretical studies I wish to give my thanks to Alexander Lipski, Douglas Osborne, Sally Falk Moore, Bruce Kapferer, and Li You-Yi and family; to trace the life accounts, of course, those participating people who gave their time, knowledge, and patience which allowed me to enter specific *culture-circles* to inspire the "search," I am grateful to the A. L. Perera family, L. K. Karunaratne and family; university colleagues who are *sangha* members, Ven. Y. Dhammapala Thero, Ven. Havanpola Ratanasara Thero, Ven. Davuldena Gnānissara Thero, Ven. Walpola Piyananda Thero, Ven. P. Sorata Thero, and Ven. Bodāgama Chandima Thero; and, Ven. Phra Maha Banyat Dhammasaro Thero in Thailand; monastery participants: Ven. Hanchapola Gnānavansa Thero, Ven. H. Seelavansa Thero, Ven. O. Chandaloka Thero, Ven. D. Rakkitha Thero, Ven. A. Ariyavansa Thero, Ven. G. Gnanatilaka Thero, and Ven. M. N. Sumanavansa Thero; *dēvāle* participants, especially H. B. Dissanayake and family; and for *gurunnānse* studies with Peemachchari Nakathige Sirineris and family; and my "Pearl Mount" family.

I appreciated the support and advice of Mr. and Mrs. G. Blundell, Gordon and Ellen Lewis, Virendra P. and Bharti Shah and their children Sandeep, Kirin, and Purvi, and Girish and Devi Veyas and family, Heddy Yeh Kuan, Merrett T. Smith and family, Richard Weisbrod, Wang J. T. and family, Lisabeth Ryder, Nalini Jayasuria, Penny Sieling, Steve Pearlman, Madelyne Gianfrancesco, Ann Walters, Hillary McElhaney, Kimberley Carr Eisenlauer, Debbie Middleton, David Okura, Michael Arlen, Karen A. Deist, Gary McGill, Ailsa Jones, A. R. (Andy) Trivedi, Sara Trivedi M. D., Raju Trivedi, Maya Trivedi, Mukundini and Mahindra Shah and family, Charles and Robin Carter and family. My special thanks go to Ch'yi Yu who originally prepared this manuscript.

*   *   *

The publishing process has been an arduous task which was a road that began while I was in Thailand as a participant in the Special Study Program on Buddhism and Thai Society, Thammasat University. Chatsumarn Kabilsingh introduced me to Suk Soongswang as a potential publisher for this book. On August 21st, 1987, Ven. Phra Maha Banyat Dhammasaro Thero and I visited Mr. Suk at his DK Book office, Bangkok. Since then, a fire disrupted Mr. Suk's plan for a Southern Asian Series. Later I contacted Michael Flamini, Acquisitions Editor, Peter Lang Publishing after a visit to the Association for Asian Studies conference in Washington, DC, 1989.

My gratitude goes to Kang Min-Ping, Hsieh Shih-Man, Dai Rai-Chuen, Chen Yu-Pei, Wu Pai-Lu, Lu Li-Chieh (Danny Lu), Huang Tai-Yi, Amanda Lin, Irene Cheng, Hsia Li-Fang, and others for their support and technical arrangement of the manuscript. I especially appreciate the patience and care of Chen Lin-Wen, research assistant of the Institute of Atomic and Molecular Sciences, Academia Sinica, and Wang Hui-Ji who is currently in the masters program of the Graduate Institute of the Department of Anthropology, National Taiwan University, for the final draft. I am grateful to Ven. Havanpola Ratanasara Thero and Punchi Banda Meegaskumbura for their re-reading and fine tuning of the text, and Brian Phillips along with Linda Wolf and Diana Garrett for reading the entire manuscript and offering suggestions to enhance the reading flow, and Jennifer Tsou who I consulted for revisions entered in 1992. Robert Waltner was able to finalize the text utilizing the Macintosh Textures system which Chen Lin-Wen set-up. Chen Lin-Wen who is now residing at the University of Cambridge e-mailed 65 missing pages and fonts. In 1993, Robert Waltner was able to craft this book together.

Upali Amarasiri, P. Vidanapathirana, Catherine Dea, Kim Seung-Hyun, Gary Seaman, and Chiang Bien gave additional bibliographic sources required to enlarge the traditional Sinhala and sociological literature. I give my appreciation to Ven. Kurunegoda Piyatissa Thero and Padmanabh S. Jaini for their recent suggestions. Thanks to them, Padmini Meegaskumbura, Barbara Waltner, Gordon Harper, Maxine Tinney, and my colleagues at National Chengchi University and National Taiwan University, including Shih Lei who patiently observed my work as my office-mate, this volume was prepared. For the publication of this book, the critical publishing responsibilities went to Joshua Phillips; Kathy Iwasaki; Christine Marra, production manager; Christopher S. Myers, managing director; and especially Nona Reuter, production supervisor, all at Peter Lang Publishing, New York. Rose Farber gave finishing assistance for the graphs. The graphic illustrations were drawn by J. David Soong and Gregory Burns, and the cover layout was completed by George Lallas. Thanks to these people this publication was accomplished.

I trust this book will serve as a guide for further cultural studies.

David Blundell

The above *indriya*, or bird's head, a Siamese
rendition, was drawn by P. C. Jinavaravaṃsa Unnānse, late Prince
Prisdand. Coomaraswamy 1956:83, *fig.* 14.

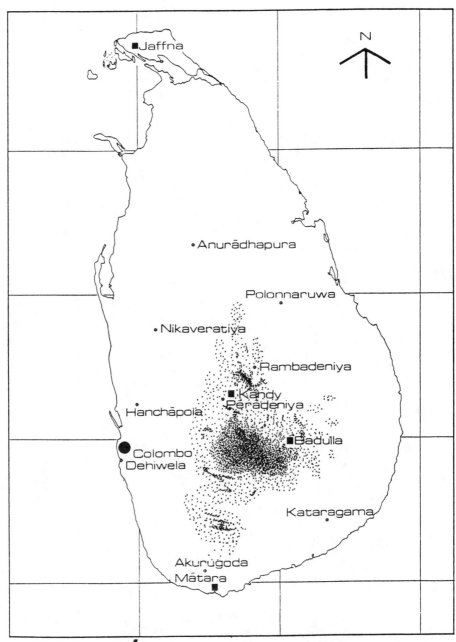

ŚRĪ LANKĀ

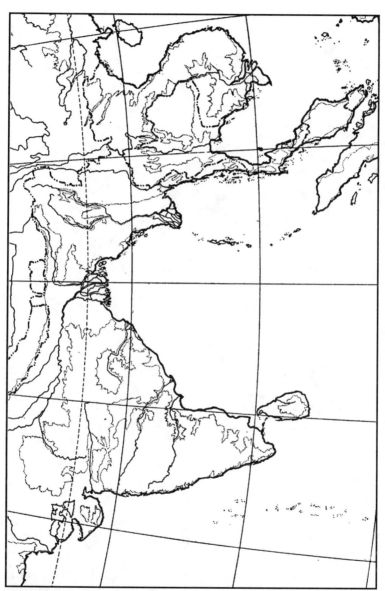

Southern Asia

A Selection from Goode's Map of Asia based on Lambert's
Equal Area Projection. © The University of Chicago

Dedicated to *Zia* which is a popular indigenous *sun* deity or emblem of New Mexico, the name of a pueblo in northern New Mexico, and the title of the Anthropology Film Center, Santa Fe, NM, USA.

Introduction

Anthropology is the scientific expression of man's curiosity about his living—not only about how other people have lived in other places and at other times, but also about how we live here and now.
                    —Robert Edgerton and L. L. Langness 1977:xi

The title *Masks* is a metaphor which represents the social role of individuals who share normative values at different levels of the Sinhalese belief system. Through the study of *persona*, one can perceive not only the social obligations which the society puts on individuals, but also the unique personalities who define their social positions. The resulting text is composed from life histories of three Sinhalese religious men presenting themselves. In this study, the three individuals were the key research participants who conveyed the facts and thoughts behind the ethnography. As a student of anthropology, I lived with these individuals to share their cultural ways according to religious specialization. Each of the research participants was "masked" according to their respective obligatory disciplines. As I progressed to a conceptual framework, I discovered that I also wore a mask as ethnographer (see Rabinnow 1982). The ethnographic presentations were composed in texts and motion pictures for Sinhalese and other audiences to observe.

This book displays my role interacting with Sinhalese participants using methodological approaches as ethnographic tools in anthropology as discussed by P. J. Pelto 1970, Robert B. Edgerton and L. L. Langness 1977, James P. Spradley 1980, and Crane and Angrosino 1992. The presented case studies are composed in various styles of research:

> The standard monograph conveys one dimension of life. Other styles of presenting ethnographic information convey different, and equally important, understandings about life in other cultures (Edgerton and Langness 1977:87).

In the multi-dimensional approach, each research tool influenced the format and outcome of the ethnographic process. In the study, the participants and I utilized motion picture as a research tool. And of course, the involved people knew that their documentation was going to be utilized as community visual presentations. The motion-picture research drew public interest and concern during the production.

In this work, *local* life writings were collected to interpret philosophical concerns, symbolic connotations, ecclesiastical modes of behavior, and

1

spontaneous actions. In all, as a heterogeneity of research associates, colleagues, and participants, we worked for the presentation of meaningful Sinhalese cultural dimensions seeking a unity on procedure.

In terms of anthropological inquiry, I agree with Clifford Geertz in stating that:

> The concept of culture I espouse...is essentially a semiotic one. Believing, with Max Weber, that man is an animal suspended in webs of significance he himself has spun, I take culture to be those webs, and the analysis of it to be therefore not an experimental science in search of law but an interpretative one in search of meaning (1973:5).

In anthropology, we must interpret the meanings that individuals give to social phenomena: "all peoples use their traditions selectively, in response to their own needs and perceptions" (Spiro 1977:239). People use their traditions as a model for constructing life in a social network. I take the approach of the individual's role in culture. Francis L. K. Hsu (1972:2) presented six points for the study of "psychological anthropology." Of the six, I will primarily deal with numbers two and three respectively: "...work that deals with the individual as the locus of culture," and "...work that gives serious recognition to culture as an independent or dependent variable associated with personality." The shared individual's experience allows communication and transaction to take place in the process of maintaining human organization.

The research approach follows the anthropological and Sinhalese systems of knowledge in order to present cultural documents within Sinhalese society.

First, I collected and presented data to represent *specific* information in various forms about the Sinhalese belief system. An economy of a method was utilized in the motion-picture production. Each scene was planned by the participants to illustrate the essence of the point and not all aspects. As Sinhalese research assistant, Conrad Ranawake, mentioned during the project work: "no use to waste film."

Second, keeping in mind the Sinhalese audience, the intention was to relate the thought process in conjunction with participants to how the data were obtained and organized utilizing the anthropological approach.

Third, in terms of approach, I followed the principle of the Rundstrom, Rundstrom, and Bergum (1973) experiment of native participant feedback to produce a cultural document as a motion picture and text, plus Jay Ruby's holistic Producer-Process-Product (1977) interactive ethnography which aims at producing reflexive presentational accounts.

Fourth, as a result of the ethnographic process, visual data were organized in a presentational format of life accounts. Motion pictures were made to re-enact events of the life's work by illustrating dance, ritual, meditation, and so on.

Fifth, therefore the procedure resulted in cultural documents with a definite source and intention for utilization in an academic setting or in public education.

The documents could be utilized in various ways as they contain verbatim—direct information (as in the case of the written life accounts) and additional visual dimensions of cultural information (details of cultural practices illustrated in the motion pictures). Much of the information was recorded to re-observe and reflect upon at a later time. The emphasis was to illustrate rather than explain, yet to allow the meaning to shine through.

The point of view reflects the research group's objective of giving information to teach about the Sinhalese culture from individuals who participate in the native belief system. If the outcome is found to be subjective, then it is because the participants are presenting what they feel to be essential information for the understanding of Sinhalese belief system dimensions.

Ethical responsibility to the Sinhalese participants and accuracy to the data are especially important in maintaining the research. *Professional Ethics: Statements and Procedures of the American Anthropological Association* (1973) originally adopted in 1971, notes that concerning "principles of professional responsibility," anthropologists should be responsible to interaction "with those studied," "to the public," "to the discipline," "to sponsors," and "to one's own government and to host governments." The ethical challenge is a commitment to veracity.

> In the final analysis, anthropological research is a human undertaking, dependent upon choices for which the individual bears ethical as well as scientific responsibility (*ibid.*:2)

The documents are not reality as such, but are real accounts portraying individuals. They are ethical truths in terms of the circles of knowledge, conditions of research, and the judgements of the participants.

In the research, there were three separate textual and audio-visual portraits, but together they represent a trilogy of the Sinhalese belief system according to the constraints and limitations of technical devices and research durations. This method is a model, any student of social sciences could follow to make a visual ethnographic portrait: (a) there is a stay for observation and social participation, (b) for the understanding of the key elements in daily life, interviews are conducted before preparing the written, oral, and photographic research, and (c) the film camera is utilized as the tool for framing life sequences.

The South Asian value system has been utilized as a means of utilizing the "emic" or indigenous approach (which to me is the meaning of "ethno-" as in *ethnographic* or *ethnography*). Douglass Price-Williams, among others (e.g., Pike 1954, Cole and Scribner 1974) distinguishes research strategies in the study of culture as two basic tendencies: *etic* and *emic*.

> The "emic" approach describes a phenomenon in terms of its own units... The "etic" approach imposes a measurement external to the phenomenon (Price-Williams 1975:23).

Price-Williams further divides his approach for cross-cultural investigation with separate categories:

1. The distinction between abstract and concrete,
2. The distinction between intellect and emotion, and
3. The distinction between rhetoric and logic, metaphor and fact. (*ibid.*:27)

In South Asian culture, the above listed distinctions are known and respected, but not always cognitively displayed at the popular level. As anthropologists attempt to define the meanings in culture, distinct references can be made in a belief system in terms of fact, process, metaphor, structure, and symbolic or linguistic form.

> One must at least have been taught to recognize equivalent symbols, e.g., rose and lotus (Rosa Mundi and Padmavati); that Soma is the "bread and water of life"; or that the Maker of all things is by no means accidentally, but necessarily a "carpenter" wherever the material of which the world is make is *hylic* (Coomaraswamy 1947:39).

Rodney Needham mentions that anthropological study isolates "primary factors," investigates "synthetic images," and standardizes operations (Needham 1978:65). In terms of symbolic or cultural interpretation, anthropologists tend to interpret symbols and rituals or myths beyond what exists. This elaborate interpreting process sometimes makes little sense to the individuals represented in the ethnography (see Jarvie 1976). In relation to contemporary Sinhalese culture, as Senake Bandaranayake (1978) stated, "...*some* symbols are just motifs without any particular meaning." Some scholars tend to enlarge meaning from symbolic interpretation. The interpretation should not overshadow the discrete cultural forms.

I have relied on the people presenting the data for relevant use as "sober description" (Schutz 1967) or "thick description" (Geertz 1973) of the recounted sequences in a life writing and motion picture. Ultimately my framing has come from the presented life account as a template encapsulating Sinhalese culture.

The Unfolding

> We must unearth human images, wherever they are to be found, so as to recognize ourselves therein.
>
> —Robert E. Meagher 1977:10

Anthropology offers the best approach in the participant observer method in crossing the analytical line to partake in the experience and then personally stepping away for the ethnographic analysis and interpretation. This methodology is what Hortense Powdermaker (1966) called "psychological involvement" with "detached objectivity."

In the interpretation and arrangement process, the ethnographer looks at appearances and connections to recognize patterns from *abstract* and *objective* forms. Subjective senses are used to assign meanings to the configuration; ethnography is never anonymous. To *see* configurations, the ethnographer observes and grows with the pattern.

The researcher must allow the spontaneous meanings to emerge from the intentional process of observation. The attention to life is the source of applied meaning, the harvesting of the patterns in the fields of human experience. The orientation "is a full-blown, actualized event, which the actor pictures and assigns to its place in the order of experiences given to him at the moment of projection" (Schutz 1967:61). The ethnographer looks carefully into the patterns in the process of life in order to distinguish life shades as coherent experiences. Only from the interpretation of retrospective observation and contemplative gaze, does discrete experiences as units of significance emerge from the study. "Meaning is merely an operation of intentionality, which however, only becomes visible to the reflective [contemplative] glance" (*ibid.*:52). Otherwise, "if we simply live immersed in the flow of [time] duration, we encounter only undifferentiated experiences that melt into one another in a flowing continuum" (*ibid.*:51). Life shades are constructed into frames by the individual reflecting on the life's experiences. The construction of the remembered life depends on the intent, and the presentation of the life into a coherent image. It depends on the interaction and skill of the one who remembers and the one who puts the remembrance into a graphic representation. In the case of autobiography, it is a process which happens in the same individual. In ethnography, the trained anthropologist usually organizes the material.

A visual ethnography operationalizes selected values in graphic form. Motion picture is not a matter of images on the eye, but a presentation in the mind which is a visual symbol with the qualities of intellectual flexibility. The primary function is to present a bracketed or framed conceptual reality. For example, Basil Wright's early motion-picture documentary *Song of Ceylon* (1934) moved away from the purely informative format to a visual essay style. Artists have presented still-photographs of Sinhalese culture as in Lionel Wendt's *Ceylon* (1950), Roloff Beny's *Island Ceylon* (1970), and *Serendip to Śrī Lankā: Immemorial Isle* (1991) by Nihal Fernando and Luxshman Nadaraja.

The life history should be presented as a single coherent image and storyline[1] such as Akemi Kikumura's book *Through Harsh Winters: The Life of a Japanese Immigrant Woman* (1981), Youngsook Kim Harvey's *Six Korean Women: The Socialization of Shamans* (1979), and the work by Robert Jay Lifton *et al.* (1979) *Six lives, Six Deaths: Portraits from Modern Japan*, or motion picture as *Bismillah Khan*, a portrait of the "prince of the *shanai* (i.e., oboe-like reed instrument)" of temple processions and marriages. But, it should be remembered that whatever is cinematic will remain theatrical; also, motion picture is based on action and aesthetics.

Why do people like *ethnographic* motion pictures? First, there is the empathic association with the human appearances on the screen. People look for qualities in the person presented which are similar to our own: the flat image becomes human. Second, there is a quality of life, shape, color, form, balance, and movement in which the very concept of stationary existence is usually abolished. Third, there is a novel form of life in a sometimes unusual setting. Fourth, there is a narrative that gives a verbal description or story. Motion picture should be dealt with as an informative art form; it does not threaten the value of written ethnography.

Motion picture was employed as a basic research tool of *motion, color, shape, form*, and *sound*. The projected image frames give a sense of motion only through the persistence of vision. It is a manipulation of physical objects and recording instruments. Each mechanical process in film making is indispensable: the camera, the film, the development and printing, the script, and the association of people who make it work. Collectively, the process was a device to identify graphic life events.

---

[1] The technique of utilizing "memories and commentaries," "oral tradition," autobiography, conversations, novels, formal biography, cross-reference life accounts, and personal memoir is illustrated by Stravinsky and Craft 1960, Vansina 1965, Brant 1969, Milton 1971, Postel-Coster 1977, Shelston 1977, Langness and Frank 1978, Kuper 1978, Lifton *et al.* 1979, and Sawada 1980.

*   *   *

The graphic life account is artificial, something abstracted from natural form. Herbert Alexander Simon's *The Sciences of the Artificial* (1969) offers "four indicia that distinguish the artificial from the natural; hence we can set boundaries..."—first, an artificial process is synthesized; second, it may imitate the appearances of natural things while lacking one or more dimensions of the reality (as a stone lion represents a real lion); third, it can be characterized by functions, goals, and adaptations; fourth, it is often a case of discussion or deliberation in its design (*ibid.*:5–6).

The case studies presented here are a dialogue between the Sinhalese participants' interpretation of their modes and motivations and my ethnographic interpretation of those life accounts. The lives are expressed according to several cultural dimensions — *sangha* (order of monks): *vihāre* (the Buddhist monastery); *basnāyaka nilamē* (chief official of the deity shrine): *dēvāle* (the shrine of the deity with its social organization); and *gurunnānse* (exorcist): *tovil maḍuva* (the made-for-the-occasion spirit shrine).

The methods utilized with the participants are vital to the understanding of the research system. Therefore, a large section deals with methodological leanings and presentational formats in terms of anthropology and the Sinhalese value system. I have sought to understand the use of drawings, sketches, audio-recordings, life account narratives—written and cinematic, and notebook procedures as performed in accordance to the sensibilities of the Sinhalese participants. This orientation is a foundation for further work in cultural life presentations. These data are arranged and analyzed in four sections:

(a) anthropological and Sinhalese circles of knowledge for the presentation of religious life accounts;

(b) life accounts as presented to me with my comments;

(c) the Sinhalese traditional health practices utilizing meditation, pilgrimage, and ritual performance;

(d) my concluding remarks, and epilogue.

Opening Note

When I was young, I travelled by mistake, but now I do it on purpose.
—Stella Benson 1929:xi

I arrived in Śrī Lankā as a college student in 1973 under the auspices of The Experiment in International Living, South Asia Program. My motivation to study among the Sinhalese people eventually stems from the warmth and kindness of a Sinhalese family in Śrī Lankā. It has been this early friendship which has promoted my studies.

From that beginning, Conrad Ranawake, a sociology student of Gananath Obeyesekere, assisted in the on-going research (1973, 1978–1979, 1980, 1981). Conrad always made the most appropriate judgement concerning the method and attitude of the research from the standpoint of socio-anthropology. Punchi Banda Meegaskumbura, lecturer of Sinhala at the University of Śrī Lankā, Peradeniya (or Peradeniya University), instructed me in language and cultural studies (1975–1976). In subsequent research, I made a motion picture for Sinhalese communities from an initial visual life account of Ven. H. Gnānavansa Thero, whose support of the process strongly influenced me to make further cultural documents.

During my monastery stay, I made several journeys in Śrī Lankā to visit other religious sites. I visited more than thirty monasteries, temples, and *dēvāles*. A *dēvāle* (deity shrine) at Badulla interested me in presenting a different aspect of the Sinhalese belief system which I had not experienced at the monastery. Also, there was another aspect to join—the dimension of the belief in spirits. In all, I felt that it was essential to experience further the various dimensions of the belief system before I could *understand* or *feel a sense of places* in the island culture.

Perspectives

The Process

Academic boundaries are artificial: the realities are the problems.

— Richard Gombrich 1971:3

The rationale for this book is twofold. First, it is designed to explain to an audience specializing in the study of culture, some salient features of stepping through *circles of knowledge* into dimensions of culture. My awareness has come from the Sinhalese people as a cultural group and specific individuals who have guided my cultural studies. Here, pains have been taken to illustrate the ethnographic process because it is important to expose the steps leading to any expertise which is based on a craft process. This outcome, in terms of the process, is a walk through the variety of inputs which I have considered from the data utilized for presentation. A Sinhalese reader should appreciate this process as a frame for understanding the underlying data such as life accounts. Second, the ethnographic material itself stands as information. It is my wish to offer a comprehensible presentation on a culture. Here, I have attempted to address the Sinhalese belief system in terms of the personal experiential knowledge of how the participants in society cope with life. Therefore, this is consciously structured in the social emic perspective—through the ethnographic process of the interacting participants—to produce case studies of specific individuals in the context of their culture. Emphasis centers on aspects of meditation, pilgrimage, and ritual performance which are related to *states of awareness in the process of living*.

The study is designed from the attitude that the ethnographer must be aware of his, or her, imposition of designs on cultural data. Yet, a structure should prevail for clarity. Reflexive questions and reservations should also prevail to make us aware that a systematic illustration of cultural dimensions is born from the thought processes of individuals struggling with the complexities of individual and collective humanness. If a format is established in the life histories or the belief system, it should be a pattern based on current intelligence—Goethe's skeptical characterization of the *Geist der Zeiten* as the historian's "own spirit in which the times are reflected" (Hughes 1958:8):

> Was ihr den geist der Zeiten heisst,
> Das ist im Grund der Herren eigner Geist,
> In dem die Zeiten sich bespiegeln.

> — "Night", Part I, *Faust*

11

The presentation and order which appear here are based on my participation in a system of knowledge which I intentionally entered to understand a South Asian belief system. This research strategy stems from first, an extensive experience at the personal-ethnographic level in the local context of each Sinhalese participant represented here; second, a collection of ideas the selected participants have about their belief system; and third, the visual, oral, and written documentation of those ideas. Whether or not, the actual belief system expressed here really is a consensual universe of ideas depends on the people interviewed, the display of their ideas in this text, and the readers' opinion of the ethnography.

The concept is that the individual in cultural context is the point of departure for the understanding of a cultural process (see the work of Radin 1913, 1920, 1926; Langness 1965; Devereux 1967; Crapanzano 1972, 1977a, 1977b, 1980; and others). In the words of George C. Homans (1967:61):

> ...the ultimate constituents of the social world are individual people
> who act more or less appropriately in the light of their dispositions and
> understanding of their situation, institution or event is the result of
> a particular configuration of individuals, their dispositions, situations,
> beliefs, and physical resources and environment.

The conversations I had with the participants were held within the context of each person's cultural life. I have used the life account approach as a key to understand in-depth perspectives of parts of the belief structure.

I treated the belief system as a whole, including its branches. That is to say, that Buddhism in Śrī Lankā is closely tied to existing beliefs in South Asia. This Buddhism is a *gloss* for classical monastic values and rules and indigenous beliefs in deities and spirits which, in some cases, overlap with the Hindu pantheon. This is the acculturated belief system which arrived and flourished under the Sinhalese kings since the time when Buddhism was established as the imperial religion of South Asia. Emperor Aśoka consolidated his war-won empire of diverse belief systems under the wisdom and logic of the Buddha. Śrī Lankā was one kingdom which accepted a royal system and, that initial Buddhism was transformed with the people, in their vicissitudes for more than twenty-two centuries.

Religious experience is a present reality even though it is based on collective history, memories, and dreams. The religious institution has confined Buddhism into a specific, yet flexible, way of realizing experience. The definitions and ways of religious experience are the factors which determine the parameters of the religion. The basic belief system as defined by Buddhists can not be confused with Hinduism even though both institutions overlap in traits and philosophy. The contrast is sometimes striking. Other times, it is a matter of philosophical gradation which makes Buddhism and Hinduism similar, as in the concept of *ahiṃsā*.

From my approach, I am defining the belief system as the religious life people observe and practice. The ideology must be observable to track and document. Therefore, the Sinhalese belief system is what the Sinhalese Buddhists practice in Śrī Lankā. That is to say, if the Sinhalese Buddhists believe in a deity cosmology and give offering and respect at the various deity shrines where both Buddhists and Hindus attend, then it is part of the Sinhalese belief system. Therefore, I have attended to the dimensions of the Sinhalese belief system at basic levels: the Buddhist monastery, the deity shrine, and at the practice of exorcism.

Within the universe of Sinhalese Buddhists, I have selected individuals who live within different social structural levels. The question should be asked: How have I arrived at these represented levels?[1] The proposition is held that the Sinhalese belief system is a unified process, but there are definable parts according to the popular levels and practices of the faith (Sinhalese Theravāda Buddhism). This does not propose that the belief system in every area has those considered levels. For that matter, there are many more (almost limitless and changing) components of the belief system. That is to say, there are many working levels in and beyond the rural Sinhalese to be explored, like the realm of Sinhalese tradesmen or Sinhalese urban dwellers, or Sinhalese educated overseas.

Personal Framework

I don't know what science is, I don't know what art is.

—Gregory Bateson
(Brand 1977:79)

The very vastness of the subject leaves a possibility that one may have something to say worth saying.

—Eliot's essay on Dante
(Fergusson 1949:7)

Writing a presentable account of one's life history is an aesthetic expression of the phenomenon of the person. Presenting the individual's own

---

[1] Scholars will separate a cultural pattern into parts to see interlocking entities. Sally Falk Moore expressed "you can theoretically cut a cultural system in so many ways" (anthropology seminar, UCLA, 1980). My separations *are* Sinhalese dimensions; although I must say Sinhalese (or for that matter, the people of any belief system) usually do not see or feel that their belief system is broken or divided into separate levels (see Moore 1975).

value is a task of human intention, intimacy, and methodological process. The ethnographer must enter a relationship with the other person for a journey into humility, respect, and sensitivity. The first priority of the relationship is an intentional commitment to mutual openness and trust. The relationship flourishes according to the known intentions of the participants. If the intentions of the relationship are properly known in advance of the research, and if the participants are faithful to their chartered interaction, then the relationship has a chance to be *just plain honest*.

I am interested in writing about lives, aesthetics, and belief systems. I chose the life history approach because it is personal and polythematic utilizing the methods which Margaret Mead (1970:246–265) called technical developments for research, including *audio-recording, filming*, and *writing*. This approach is a kind of deductive structuralism. That is to say, if structuralism in anthropology takes a logical priority of the whole over its parts (i.e., a study utilizing some network relationship system to understand its components), I will start and end with the individual's own stories and ideas as a human identity in the system from basic levels; although I believe that the overarching structure exists. My approach is based on synchronic emphasis to a specific reference point indicated by place and time, although the life accounts are certainly diachronic. In the temporal aspect of life, the various stages of life must be stopped and framed in order to observe the individual's pattern.

Because the life process is multi-dimensional, the final representation already implies and carries multi-dimensional symbolic interpretations and meanings. What a person believes to be a complete logical life process is illusory. There are no absolute verifications of the individual's input and output except the life process itself seems logical according to the observer's own *mental map*:

> We are what we think
> All that we are arises with our thoughts
> With our thoughts we create the world

> —Buddha
> (Byrom 1976)

The entire ethnographic research displays the values of the individuals who related their life patterns to me. This is a matter of ethnographic method and ethical respect.

For a reasonable understanding of an individual, the ethnographer should have a background in psychology and anthropology; or, at least an awareness of psychological and cultural processes. In terms of psychology, the writer should be aware of the mental modes of "symbolic" consciousness: first, the waking state of world events and actions; and second, the unconscious state of intuition, dreams, feelings, introspection, meditation, the intention of being, trance and various stages of so called *altered states*. The waking and the unconscious states compose the personal aesthetic sense of an individual. Therefore, the total psychological aspects of an individual call for the arrangement of some aesthetic dimension which is idiosyncratic, yet utilized in a cultural context. The cultural connection forms the personal configuration into a figure presentable within that culture. The individual/cultural dimensions share an aesthetic which are complementary.

Each of the participants in my study is a man balanced with religious values and intellectual knowledge of the faith, either from education at various levels or by direct experience in the practice of that faith. As religion is a fluid and changing institutional entity, so each man represented in the life accounts learned to cope with changing conditions.

Ethnographic Encounter

No relationship significantly entered can ever end—the trouble is with the significant entry.

— David Cooper 1974:113

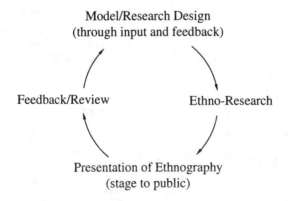

Model/Research Design
(through input and feedback)

Feedback/Review   Ethno-Research

Presentation of Ethnography
(stage to public)

The above illustration represents the cycle of the research.

Model of Research Design

When ethnographers study other cultures, they must deal with three
fundamental aspects of human experience: what people do [cultural
behavior], what people know [cultural knowledge], and the things people
make and use [cultural artifacts].

—James P. Spradley 1980:5

A research strategy depends upon what the researcher wishes to explain at a certain time; the researcher's personal background; and the crite-
ria and methods used in the study. In multi-dimensional research, the first
activity is to imagine. This occurs and changes according to the researcher's
reflective thought processes. Jerome S. Bruner (1973) stated imagining is
to "go beyond the information given." The ethnographic act is to focus
precisely into human imagination and construct an acceptable image moving from subject to style, and style to method. The mental image must be
resolved as an open graphic representation for public vision to be placed
in the social manifestation of reality (see Berger and Luckmann 1967). In
other words, ideas become modeled in eventual space and time as art or
thesis for the public to *observe* and *comprehend*. Visions residing as idiosyncratic references to the imaginer remain as conjectures and dreams of
the uninitiated person, until he or she is socialized. This occurs in forms of
writing about it, or "constructing" it for the public (social group) to observe
and experience. Then the idiosyncratic thought process becomes actualized
as a part of the collective system, known and expressed by society. The
presentation of internalized thought is based largely on the external world
in terms of form (i.e., what a person experiences or observes in daily life—
the environment) and interpersonal activities, such as communication and
feedback. The resulting image-forms are almost universal (cross-cultural),
but the variations and meanings are infinite and gradual. Models are the
graphic representation of the imagination. The validity of their forms rely
on social consensus.

Ethnographic Research

Anthropological field work is conducted by the repeated performance of
five fundamental tasks: watching, asking, listening, sometimes doing,
and recording.

—L. L. Langness 1965:3

The actual research, or the process of ethnography is a personal endeavor among people. The researcher will try to study people in association
with participants of the culture of research. I believe anthropological study
is a *contract* between the researcher and the participants of the research. At

the time of research, the participants and researcher work in cooperation for shared knowledge. *A study includes everyone who participates*, so all are influenced by their *degree* of participation. In my experience, a mutual contract (written of otherwise) is agreed upon by those persons involved as a statement regarding:

(a) the motivation of the research,

(b) the method and approach of the research,

(c) the selected tools used in the research,

(d) the duration of research time,

(e) the quality of skills held by the participants for doing the research,

(f) the expected outcome of the research,

(g) the eventual display and use of the outcome and related material obtained during the research process.

Indeed research expectations are strange. When someone expects a certain quality in the performance of the research, then those expectations should be met or changed so that what is being done, in terms of the research, is acceptable to the participants. A research design is a formal statement; but, it should have *built-in* alternatives for flexibility if unforeseen events take place.

In the case of my research topic, all intentions were discussed from the beginning. Every interested person had the chance to read or discuss the format and projected outcome of research. All names of individuals and places were used. The process of the research took the programmed course; and, if there was any change in the format, responsible individuals informed all others personally or by public communication.

This research began in 1979 as a life account motion picture of a head-monk; and then from 1980 it was expanded by the suggestion of Conrad Ranawake to include the life account of a *basnāyaka nilamē* (deity shrine chief)[1], and an exorcist in 1981. I followed the same pattern as the 1979 research, including an array of three separate life accounts. Each research step was unique, as the time and situation presented various parameters. For example, the headmonk's research was done in a monastery, where I recorded the happenings and the historical life in a span of several study

---

[1] Deity shrines (*dēvāles*) are found in many parts of Śrī Lankā. Some highly influential figures have been promoted and recognized as *dēvatās* by the people of respective areas. In order to pay respect and receive their blessings devoted persons have erected (*dēvāles*). At times, royal patronage was received by them. Land-grants were given to some important (*dēvāles*).

months. The *basnāyaka nilamē* research took place during a number of coming-in and going-out of the field occasions because I did not live in the *dēvāle*, as with my stay in the monastery. Then, the exorcist research was handled in a short field season in 1981; just in and around the exorcist's home. In every case, "validity" was assured by the careful guidance of Punchi Banda Meegaskumbura (teacher of Sinhala and methodology) and Conrad Ranawake (sociologist and researcher).

I will briefly review my format of research. First, an extended duration of stay to understand the daily happenings. Second, a still camera was used to photograph key scenes for analysis. Third, life accounts and stories were informally collected. Fourth, still photographs were placed in a story board format for visual presentation and discussion of the ethnographic layout. Fifth, a motion-picture treatment or script was written for each agreed-upon scene. Sixth, the motion-picture camera was placed "in front" of each happening, and a discussion of the content during and after filming (the process of motion-picture camera work). Seventh, ethnographic film footage was selected by the research group.

Presentation of Ethnography

The next step in the ethnography process was the presentation, or the staging to the public, of ethnographic material. The ethnography was externalized according to Sinhalese aesthetics. I am interested in the presentation of thoughts and graphic forms communicated not only within a society, but cross-culturally as well. It is the point of the task for the writer, artist, or dramatist, to piece together thoughts into a coherent whole for other people to taste. The coherent expression of experience is the aesthetic aspect of the research.

Ananda Coomaraswamy (1922) posited the view that the scientist of the Western disciplines and the craftsman of the Asian disciplines share a common tendency of conceptual orientation for qualified aesthetic/technical procedure:

> The comparison of Eastern art with [Western] science is likewise well-considered: for like the scientist, the Oriental craftsman aims at explicit demonstration rather than elegant procedure, and the intrusion of personal taste is to be avoided in art as the intrusion of personal bias is avoided in science. In setting forth the stories of heroes, or making the images of gods, the Asiatic craftsman has no thought of art, as we now understand the word. The primary qualification demanded of him [or

her] was obedience: [as] he [the artist] was not required to be a creature of moods, but to know his trade [as craft] (*ibid.*:i).

This Śrī Lankā scholar continued his point by saying that adherence to skill and discipline was the theme of the tradition. Oriental art, moreover, is not an escape from life, nor an interpretation of life having any peculiar tendency: it is a part of life itself in the same sense as the art of preparing a meal or designing a motor car. It is thus entirely without affection and securely founded in real experience.

> "Fine Art," on the contrary, is a refinement upon life, and by no means inherent in life itself—if it were otherwise it would be apparent in our streets, our costume, kitchen utensils, churches, and department stores. We have learnt to speak of "art for art's sake," and to leave it out of our daily life, precisely as we make of religion a Sunday observance, and leave it out of our banking and making love (*ibid.*:ii–iii).

This is not to say that Asian arts are a rigid display of the culture and not the individual. Certainly basic individual traits come through the traditional art.

An example of the use of traditional art in literature is the account of the "Pageant of Śrī Lankā," which was written as a vocal play in the *Independence Vesak* number (1947) to commemorate the history and people of Śrī Lankā (i.e., the Sinhalese).[2] A publication by W. R. McAlpine (1980) entitled *A Vesak Oratorio: The Birth, Enlightenment and Passing Away of the Buddha* is a fine example of poetic style. An excerpt of this writing, from this diplomat who was the Representative of the British Government in Śrī Lankā from 1968 to 1974 (retired in Śrī Lankā since 1975), is given below to illustrate this written impression.

The Buddha

The noble wisdom streams through me.
Truth arises with its bliss and blessed
Delight comes forth.
I am boundless in joy
And in that joy my heart is stayed.

---

[2] Buddhist writing has a literary heritage of about 2,300 years in South Asia. For recent works which give illustrative presentational translations of texts: Guenther 1969, Wray *et al.* 1972, Trungpa 1975, Cone and Gombrich 1977, Amore and Shinn 1981. As for the Pāli of Śrī Lankā consult Malalasekera (1958) *The Pāli Literature of Ceylon.*

Chorus

O dawn of dawnings!
We wake from dark, we rise from sleep.
We walk in the way of Your light.
We bathe in the waters of Your joy and compassion.
We wash in the river of Your love and serenity.
In the cool of Your cave we go to find refuge,
In the calm of Your court we go to find shelter.
O man made perfect and pure!
Down the days of the turn of the sun,
Down the nights of the full of the moon,
We shall do honour, we shall give praise to Your name,
With flowers at the peace of Your lotus feet.

Narrator

Under the bō-tree that shelters His wisdom,
He remains in the majesty of meditation poise,
As He will be known and forever remembers:
Carved in rest, shaped in peace, cast in eternity.

A Voice

The petals of the lotus flower unfold
To bare a deathless form, where time unites
Past, present, future in a timeless mould,
A universe distilled in stainless light.
Benign the touch of smile upon the lips,
The arms reposed, the fingers formed in grace.
The nightless brow unshackled silent sits
Amid extinction of the worldly face.

—W. R. McAlpine 1980:58

In the above passage, the Buddha spoken of here was in the last watch of the night of his enlightenment. It is mentioned that he was under the *bō*-tree and the narrator describes the Buddha in terms of the distinguished granite images—as the Buddha statue was expressed in living stone at Galvihāre, Polonnaruwa, 12th Century (Wikramagamage 1991).

In terms of Śrī Lankā, there are a number of "secular" autobiographical accounts. I will mention two notable accounts in the English language: In 1660 Robert Knox was shipwrecked on the coast and he managed to reach the highlands of the country, the Kandyan Kingdom, where he remained for about twenty years. After that time he wrote an account of the people and nature of the highlands while on his return voyage to England. The preface read in the English of that time: "An Historical Relation of the Island Ceylon in the East-Indies: together With an Acount of the Detaining in Captivity the Author and divers other Englishmen now Living there..." It is a detailed exposition of island life.

Another famous account is an autobiography *An Asian Prime Minister's Story*, written by Sir John Kotelawala (1956), describing his modest beginnings and how he reached the position of prime minister for the newly independent nation. In the account, the reader observes that the author is highly influenced by the English, but as a national leader he explains that he retains the independent voice of a Sinhalese man.

In my research, I have displayed the data to the participants for "aesthetic" and "valid" evaluation. The research was commented upon by the participants and colleagues for sections to be retained or changed.

Feedback/Review

Men do not reason often; they do not reason for long at a time; and when they do reason they are not very good at it.
—Rodney Needham 1978:69

In the reflection of ethnographic material, access to research should be open to consulting colleagues in the discipline for feedback in the actualization process of the research. At each stage of fieldwork, I consulted with local scholars of Sinhalese culture (e.g., Punchi Banda Meegaskumbura), and colleagues in the discipline of anthropology wrote letters to assist in the thought process. Professors Maquet and Langness advised me to consider the qualitative aspect of the research in terms of the cultural environment (as in the monastic/spatial attitudes of the monks in relation to the temple) and life accounts. Don and Sue Rundstrom wrote to me while I was in Śrī Laṅkā as participants in the feedback process. Their letters gave me additional information on the film tracking process of the research. The guidance lines sent by the Rundstroms are given as the following "pointers":

(a) Separate community *circles of knowledge* influence one another. Tracking these influences is important as the research progresses. Most projects fall short in this endeavor.

(b) The question of validity and reliability of your information must hold up to examination, regardless of which way you choose to go in terms of your theoretical and conceptual tools or framework.

(c) Apply photograph interviewing to discern categories and "contextual" relations that are verbal or extend that need to move into the visual mode.

(d) Obtain consent or "releases" for field information in order to cover the participants.

Feedback must come into effect and be continuous in the effort to record the study. The participants involved must understand what is going on and the eventual outcome of the work. Then the tentative life history document should be shown to the participants for *open discussion* to maintain, direct, or redirect the work. This is to open or expose the material to the organic process of mutual feedback for its integrity and genuineness. Thus, the work should not evolve in a vacuum of scholarly purpose. It should be cross-referenced with a variety of input and feedback for a working consensus on the social construct of objectivity. In my opinion, anthropology was founded, and should be committed to, the method of mutual trust and respect of the views expressed by the people intimately involved. Actually, does the eventual written life history end as it becomes structured and displayed in a format? In the life of a person, it is a re-interpreting and re-defining process. Since the life account is only a *reflection* at a point in time, it is a mental dwelling place.

Ethnographic feedback must be sought when the process is complete, to observe if the research into public process actually comes to its mark of authenticity. This last act is the critical test to determine the *effectiveness* of the ethnography going public. Once the reviews of the presentation are received, then the ethnographer can relate to what people comprehend about the ethnography in terms of the original concept.

The research cycle is complete when the associated group of that particular ethnography, the discipline, and the public at large have learned something useful in cultural knowledge. The audio-recordings, films, and writings have different uses—and they should be put to efficient demonstration. For this work, the participants of the research, my academic committee, and to some extent an external audience have had some access to the presentable ethnography, especially in the form of motion picture, for a review of the material.

Feedback or response to the ethnography is very important for the final analysis of the work. Again, the participants in the research should involve themselves in the review of the recorded and presented material. In terms of the present research, feedback was an essential assessment to the success or failure of the presented material—as the presentations were made for the Sinhalese participants and their community.

Valid "If"

The test is to subject the work to the people from whom the work was written about.

—Hilda Kuper 1982

Validity means competent and ethical truth. People believe things to be true if the information matches reasonable circumstances of their society. If an exorcist performs a ceremony for an ailing man, and the man recovers—it is a *fact* that the man recovered after the ritual; an implication that the exorcist's performance had something to do with the man's recovery. This is not to say that people necessarily believe the exorcist is solely responsible for the recovery. This is what Martin Southwold terms as "symbolically true" or "If people regard a presentational symbol—more especially a tenet—as having a 'fitting' or 'appropriate' relation to reality, I say they regard it as 'symbolically true'" (Southwold, 1979b:636). Southwold separates what is symbolically true with what he terms as what people "hold as factually true"..."though [he says] the two are easily and often confused" (*ibid*). The reader of Southwold gets the feeling that ideological truth is different from the usual factual truth as it is understood according to science:

It is enough, first to acknowledge that ritual symbols—including tenets, belief, dogmas—do convey conceptions about reality, and hence may be regarded as true or false (*ibid.*).

True things (or *truths*) are symbolically accepted to be what they are: a kind of reality. This "fitting" or "appropriate" relation to reality (*ibid.*) is just that: a relationship. It should be evident that the verb "believe" designates a *relation* rather than a *state*: a relation, first between the believer and a proposition, and second from the believer through the proposition to reality (see *ibid.*:638). How does a researcher present another way of life in terms of the "emic" point of view so that an audience from another culture will understand it? In this research, I have essentially made motion pictures *with*, and *by* three individuals for their own use to show at home. Certainly the outcome of the films and the life histories has been influenced by the methods employed in the research.

Ethnographic Model, Context, and Individual

> The methodologies of all true sciences are rational, involving, as they
> do, the use of formal logic and interpretive schemes.
>
> — Alfred Schutz 1967:240

Anthropological Studies in Theravāda Buddhism[1] is the title of Cultural Report Series No.13, Southeast Asia Studies, Yale University, 1966. In this report, Nash, Obeyesekere, Ames, and Moerman, among other social anthropologists, wrote on the state of the Buddhist belief system common to Śrī Lankā and Southeast Asia:

> ...as studies on Buddhism they confront an established tradition of
> historical and textual scholarship; and as studies of the relations of
> religion and society they explore and venture into a large region of
> philosophical uncertainty (Nash 1966:vii).

Manning Nash cites three kinds of fieldwork in the anthropological articles which I believe to be the fine point of departure to express as a standard for ethnography: "First, the basis [of ethnography] is the writer's own observations, made during a protracted residence among the people reported on... The second, growing out of the first, is that the reports are on bounded,

---

[1] Theravāda Buddhism is the "overarching" belief system in Śrī Lankā, Thailand, Burma, Laos, and Cambodia. Theravāda means the "voice of the elders" which preserves the wisdom of the Buddha for generations. In the 1st Century B.C., the sayings were written in Pāli and then edited and commented upon for the next two millennia.

For further studies in contemporary Theravāda Buddhist traditions see Leach 1962, Spiro 1970, Tambiah 1970, Obeyesekere 1972, Lester 1973, Ferguson 1975, Swearer 1981, Collins 1982, Gothóni 1982, and Gombrich and Obeyesekere 1988. In terms of general Buddhism see Arnold 1879, Thomas 1927, Soni 1945, Humphreys 1956, Basham 1959, Conze 1959, Gard 1961, Jayasuriya 1963, Jayatilleke 1963, Ven. Narada 1964, Schecter 1967, Govinda 1969, Hayashima 1969, Ven. Nyanaponika 1975, Kalupahana 1976, Yoo 1976, Southwold 1983, Harvey 1990, and Payne 1991.

Sources of belief system theories, methods, and accounts for this study include Oman 1903, McCabe 1912, Allport 1950, Laski 1961, Ven. Rahula 1956, James 1960, Mandelbaum 1964, Geertz 1966, de Waal Malefijt 1968, Kennedy 1969, Obeyesekere 1972, Smart 1973, Beidelman 1974, Dolmatoff 1975, Moore 1975, Malalgoda 1976, Lessa and Vogt 1979, Maslow 1981, and Dumézil 1988.

25

named, and real societies or social systems... All...show an awareness of the fact that their unit of study forms but part of a large social and cultural system... Third, [they manifest] the anthropologists' emphasis on comparison" (*ibid.*:vii). But, Gananath Obeyesekere states "Yet it is all too easy to make the mistake of translating a set of methodological assumptions into empirical 'facts'" (Obeyesekere 1966:1).

Views on Facts

"Facts" include a person's interpretation of sensory input... meaning is a combination of the individual's interpretation and the objective patterns or forms apprehended.

—Gerardus van der Leeuw 1938:59

Culture is an integrated process through which people identify themselves in relation to a pattern of life histories, experiences, actions, and artifacts. Individuals develop in the process of cultural configuration to stage ideas, satisfy body requirements, and fulfill intellectual, entertainment, and social interests. People translate their world according to the "social facts" rendered in the social collectivity of ideas. Participation in a belief system gives the person authenticity in the context of the established institutional norms of behavior. Social authority characterizes the person with a public image: a social *persona*. Accounts in ethnography usually consider socially identified facts according to a human system of expectations which have become institutionalized as a force of roles.

The concept of *social facts* as a research device was presented by Émile Durkheim just less than a century ago. Durkheim's term is used to classify the things of social enquiry from the standpoint "that (a) institutions are generally quite independent of the particular individuals who occupy roles within them, and (b) the important characteristics of the human personality presuppose, logically and causally, the existence of a social content" (Gellner 1965:655). The philosophy of Durkheim was to propose that phenomena should be a matter of strict procedural investigation as science. In Durkheim's words, "The first and most fundamental rule is: *consider social facts as things*" (Durkheim 1966:14). Durkheim included the humanities within the realm of disciplined Western science.

Émile Durkheim and Max Weber saw the extent of social forces on the individual and accepted the dimension as "facts." But, they also explained that social forces were necessary as a social condition in which the individual grew in terms of self and public control or disciplined social welfare, and spiritual belonging (see Streng 1969:43).

The importance of social facts comes in the trend of "common man" studies in contrast with the historic "great social men" studies featuring "famous" individuals as (by historians primarily) influencing large institutions. In the 20th Century, perhaps, there is an over interest in the individual in terms of the consequences of vast government and private corporations. But, certainly the "industrial and political revolutions" of the Eighteenth and Nineteenth centuries placed the "common man" in a democratic position of "worth" and social consequence. The overall decline of the royal world and the rise of the business enterprise or socialist orientation of commodities has created a "Protestant" or republic age image of individuals living in an "age of human rights." The institutions flexed and transformed as the society changed and adapted to new trends. *Social facts* are useful tools in defining data for charting the ways and means of social institutions.

George E. G. Catlin, in his "Preface" to the second edition to Émile Durkheim's *The Rules of Sociological Method* (1966:1), wrote:

> Myths, popular legends, religious conceptions of all sorts, moral beliefs, etc., reflect a reality different from the individual's reality; but the way in which they attract and repel each other, unite or separate... they would behave in their mutual relations as do sensations, images, or ideas, in the individual.

The individual personality fits into the network of social institutions: a larger complex of moral ideas, images, and attitudes. Institutions allow altered behavior to some specialized individuals (e.g., exorcists and artists) and to the public at large in ritual occasions (e.g., marriage ceremonies, pilgrimage journeys, and religious events). Durkheim's method emphasizes the "social solidarity" of the individuals but, by the same token it recognizes the importance of individual human personality.

> A whole is not identical with the sum of its parts. It is something different, and its properties differ from those of its component parts. ...society is not a mere sum of individuals. Rather, the system formed by their association represents a specific reality which has its own characteristics (Durkheim 1966:102–103).

Durkheim expressed that the human sciences should establish relations of causality and conceptual understandings to things. In science, as in other belief systems, a duality existed between concept and fact. A belief system uses a technical language to conceptualize reality; and, a belief system, religious or scientific, depends on levels of faith.

Conceptual Levels

The first article in every creed is the belief in salvation by faith.

—Emile Durkheim 1965:464

Hans-Dieter Evers (1972) presents a social/structural kind of triad in his *Monks, Priests and Peasants* concerning the case study of the Rajamahavihāraya Lankātilaka in the Kandyan highlands. According to Evers, three religious economic and political interdependent levels have developed in the belief system: the monastic *vihāragam* held by monks, the *dēvāle* holdings (*dēvālagama*), and the royal lands (*gabaḍāgam*) of lordship and peasant tenure. The social structure of the *vihāre* in the case study certainly matches that model, but the arrangement misses the workings of spirits in the system. That is because Evers is only analysing a temple and its social structure in terms of the "great tradition." If the researcher includes the society at large, then Ever's three basic partitions must have additional wings and tiers. In my opinion, the *vihāre* institution was rightly placed in the schematic exercise. But, the *dēvāle* and the royal palace (i.e., *māligāva*) or even the *vihāre* and the royal palace really compose an elite unit: the "Radiant Great Royal Temple" or the *beauty-spot* of Lankā.

In theoretical temple categories, Senake Bandaranayake divides the great temple monasteries of ancient Anurādhapura into functioning aspects of the triple-gem Buddha-Dhamma-Saṅgha. The "threefold architectural division" protected the enshrined relics and symbolic holy representations of the Buddha, e.g., *cetiya* or *dāgäba* (Paranavitana 1988), ecclesiastical buildings facilitated congregational functions of the *sangha* and laity usually for the dissemination of the *dhamma* (i.e., words of the Buddha), and the residential structures provided for the monk's living and eating space (Bandaranayake 1974:27–28). The temple structure is an ideational model usually set-up as a Buddhist rural temple (see Klausner 1964, Moerman 1966, Maquet 1975a, and Gothóni 1982).

Michael Ames introduces his article "Ritual Presentations and the Structure of the Sinhalese Pantheon," (1966:27) by stating:

> When anthropologists turn to the study of religion they seem to emphasize either psychological or cultural aspects. Religion is viewed as the source of a series of projective, cathartic, and adjustive mechanisms on the one hand or as a system of quasi-linguistic symbols, value orientations, and world views on the other. In either case the social structure of the religious community usually receives only passing notice.

Ames' (1966:28) point of departure is that "the 'structure' of the Sinhalese pantheon ('certain aspects of myth') is a direct reflection of the arrangement of ritual presentations ('certain aspects of ritual')." This follows the

Durkheim proposition that there is a real symbiosis between the deities and people and "without offerings and sacrifices they [both] would die" (Durkheim 1965:38). The "mirror image" of myth and ritual is not perfect, as Ames points out, but there is a resemblance in terms of structure.

Tripartition

Social structure is the body, technology is the tool.

—Li, You-Yi 1982

Tripartition is an "etic" macrodynamic perspective abstract of the society because it is not on the "daily mind" of the people. It is a model that indigenous and foreign scholars have constructed in order to chart the belief system. In a similar way, Sinhalese historians have partitioned Sinhalese history into traditional epochs to include Early Anurādhapura, Anurādhapura, Late Anurādhapura, Polonnaruwa, Kandyan Kingdom, Colonial, and Independent. These time frames or cuts have been constructed from archaeological/historical literary evidence of civilization change. The actual course of time had no such frames. Buddhism has its "etic" and "emic" categories. The macrodynamic categories are based on holistic institutional beliefs. The microdynamic view of society, on the other hand, is one of personal touch inspired in the quest of having individual experience. It is an immediate way of thinking and coping with a fluctuating world of temporal limits: as we live only so long to know the phenomenon of life. The "emic" unit for the microdynamic view is the individual life.

The believers of *truth* are the people who embrace the mainstream rules and categories, and there are individuals holding various other or "eccentric" frames of reference which are integrated to some degree holistically. In Southern Asia the believers fall into a vast spectrum of categories of religious and ethnic groups. The tendency of the "etic' Hindu/Islamic diverging view points partitioned South Asia in 1947.

The legacy of this "etic" view comes under the heading of *world view*, principle, intention, and governing style which look reasonable to most *indigenous eyes* as legitimate; any paradox falls away to the level of one system. The model comes to surface under the research of scholars who present the legitimate or various forces of the persisting social structure.

In terms of the Sinhalese belief system, I am not convinced there is any special way it should be cut for academic enquiry (i.e., the concept of the Great Tradition and Little Tradition dyad seems to separate formal philosophical Theravāda Buddhism [the tradition of the elders] from the multiplicity of "local" belief variations). Richard Gombrich (1971) presents his *Precept and Practice: Traditional Buddhism in the Rural Highlands of Ceylon* as a study of an "orthodox or syncretistic" belief system in question. Martin Southwold (1982) in his article "True Buddhism and Village Buddhism in Śrī Lankā," imposes a difference as the ideal faith and the local interpretation of the philosophy. The dyad is an operational approach to a civilization and its components. Gananath Obeyesekere states that the difference between village and "great" traditions or societies implies a binary orientation (i.e., "half-society," "half-culture"). According to Obeyesekere (1966:2), this model does not qualify components of a multi-variant system:

> Sinhalese Buddhism, though based on the Great Tradition, is not its equivalent and can be conveniently thought of as a "Little Tradition" [see Redfield 1956]... The Little Traditions of Southeast Asia "Theravāda" societies differ from one to another: their Great Traditions are the same [structure].

Although there is an overarching international philosophy of Theravāda Buddhism, the separate countries have their own component identities:

> Sinhalese Buddhism as I approach it will not be viewed as a composite structure consisting of several strata or systems within systems but as a unitary tradition amenable to systemic differentiation (*ibid.*).

H. L. Seneviratne (1961) declares Gananath Obeyesekere was the first to express the concept of a "Sinhalese religion" or belief system as it is applied to Buddhism in Śrī Lankā. Gananath Obeyesekere states that the Sinhalese belief system is village or "locally institutionalized." I agree that the local belief system is unitary—and ultimately connected to the larger network of the "national" Sinhalese belief system. The unitary structure is evidently present, but there are components or dimensions definable for theoretical purposes.

Gananath Obeyesekere (1966) has presented a *diagram* of the Sinhalese world as specified by the Rambadeniya community pantheon (on the next page). He points out that the basic model resembles the national Sinhalese belief system. In his presentation, the system of Buddha, and guardian deities of Śrī Lankā represent the upper side of a triangle point; and the district lesser-deities "demons," and host of spirits at the base of the triangle, represent a universal Sinhalese system. A similar system can be found in other contemporary writings of Sinhalese scholars. Lynn de Silva (1980) in *Buddhism: Beliefs and Practices in Śrī Lankā* proposes the pattern of a divine triad in culture: the Buddha, guardian deities, and local spirits. It is based on the institutions that follow the sequence: first, the *saṅgha* (order of monks) equals the direct moral obligation to the code of the Buddha (as the Great Sage or enlightened monk); second, the *dēvāle* (deity shrine) is

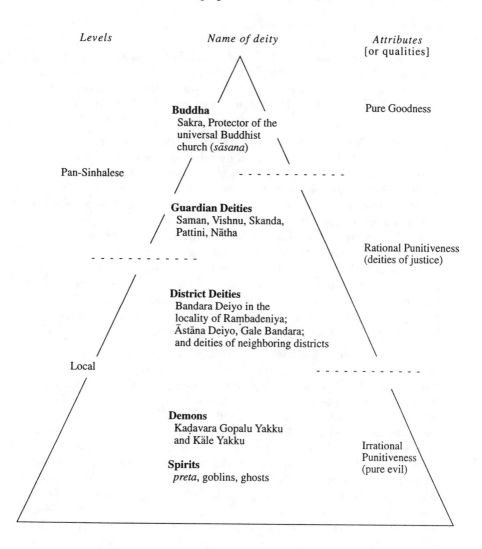

Adapted from G. Obeyesekere 1966:6

where rituals are held for the celestial beings who are interested in human activities and the protection of the nation of Śrī Lankā; and third, the institution of spirit cosmology as manifest in human/spirit health care (e.g., *tovil* and other specialized ritual performances). This *tripartition* fits into a larger scheme of theories: Such as, the Georges Dumézil theory of Indo-European belief systems.[2] The Dumézil concept of tripartition has received notable mention in recent years (Littleton 1966, see Dumézil 1988).

Georges Dumézil bases his approach on the basic structure of the social hierarchy of Indo-Europeans. The dimensions of the belief system fit into levels based on linguistic clues and ancient literary mythological themes. Dumézil even finds comparisons in herd behavior in the mythologies of European and South Asian cultures. The Dumézil tripartition should be seen as a dynamic operating in constant change as society changes, yet some salient feature are retained as a social thread in the course of time. The binary aspect occurs in tripartition as human oppositions occur when there is encounter and conflict. But, somehow the balance resumes in a three way position. For example priests and warriors/rulers might come into conflict, but eventually they will work out their differences or a third force (the merchants) will take advantage of the situation to assert themselves for a better position. Three factors are the norm according to South Asian logic.

Georges Dumézil's form of tripartition stems from the three *Ārya* castes of northern South Asia. According to Dumézil, from the beginning of the Indo-European speaking people living on the Ganges plain, there was a social organization of *brahaman* such as the orthodoxy of priests; *ksatriya* such as warriors; and *vaiśyas* such as cultivators of the land. A fourth caste known as the *śūdras* were the scheduled non-Ārya people who were perhaps mostly "indigenous." This system of social stratification was also reflected in the realm of deities mentioned in the *Reg Veda* hymns. Such a pattern seems to be simplified as Dumézil moved beyond his realm of knowledge into the past with limited evidence to lay a theoretical foundation of vast dimensions. But, it does allow for an overarching structure with a common linguistic background. The assumptions are great and the hypothesis is difficult to prove in any accurate way. Dumézil was a specialist in Indo-European (the proposed source language for the Indo-European language family) and he was a generalist in terms of applying a linguistic basis for the

---

[2] Littleton (1966:17) points to the Greek Ionian "tribes" which consisted of priests and magistrates, warriors, labors, and artisans which perhaps is similar to or stems from the original Indo-European social pattern. For a further tripartition source see John Brough (1959) "The Tripartition Ideology of the Indo-Europeans: An Experiment in Method."

understanding of a prevailing and far-reaching social organization. Some scholars have tried to prove Indo-European theories on the basis of specialized scholarship and other specialists have attempted to find weakness where Dumézil went beyond the evidence into the unknown.

In Śrī Lankā, the Indo-European tendency of tripartition has not embraced the caste system (as the cultivators are the highest caste). The Sinhalese belief system is similar to a triad in terms of overall divisions: (1) *Buddha* sphere, (2) *Dēva* sphere, and (3) *Bhūta* sphere (Meegaskumbura 1983).

> The Thai case is similar to those of Śrī Lankā and Burma in that Buddhism maintains a paramount position within a complex religious situation. ...I distinguish three components in Thai religion...: Buddhism, a Brahmanistic component, and an animistic component (Kirsch 1977:241).

The Thai example of the complexity of the belief system is a profound case which correlates with the case of Dumézil in Śrī Lankā as well as the other Theravāda countries in Southeast Asia. Kirsch states that the Thai belief system is:

> ...syncretic, in which elements derived from several historically discrete traditions have combined to form a single distinctive tradition. In such a situation, individuals [urban or rural] may simultaneously hold belief or practice rituals derived from different traditions, without any apparent sense of incongruity (*ibid.*).

In this view, Kirsch compares the European bias of the "intricate mix of indigenous and non-indigenous elements...a situation in which tolerance exists for a competition among a number of distinct and autonomous faiths [e.g., Christianity or Islam] for the religious adherence of the populace" (*ibid.*). From my research, I accept this concept of the syncretic whole system rather than a competitively divided one. But also I believe that there are elements that compose the whole: such as the Thai "indigenous-animist, Brahmanic, Buddhist" (*ibid.*:242). As Kirsch suggested in 1977, it will be the "structural/functional" approach that explores the relationship of the elements composing a complete system. This approach understands the belief system in the ethnoghraphic present.

Certainly any broad generalization is only a *manifesto*—not to be confused with specific details of a culture under the purview of the theory. Tripartition fits the Sinhalese structure as a *useful device* as Durkheim's *social facts*. Therefore, tripartition is a useful working model of the social structure. A grand hypothesis can only serve as an overall model for a larger vision of how the social system operates.

In the belief system, forms and processes of greater or lesser power are not isolated for worship, but they are in relationship to each other. The relationships are the key to understand the human system which is based on social relationship. The special attributes of each deity is a function in the relationship; and the belief system or systems operate by a human sharedness. The separateness of the belief systems stems from a particular orientation to the faith (set of beliefs) or deity. In Śrī Lankā, the Buddhists are Buddhists, yet they share the so-called Hindu deities which have in essence entered the Sinhalese belief system. Of course, the ideal plan of a particular belief system is simpler than the actual system of relationships (Gunawardana 1979).

The belief system in Śrī Lankā among the Sinhalese is a three dimensional network with vertical and horizontal aesthetic balance. The apex is represented by the Buddha and then the down flow covers a host of rational and good spirits in the vast dimensions of the irrational and evil local spirits. The religious system interlocks with Hindu dynamic formation that proclaims a scheme of high deities which come after the Buddha in the Sinhalese system. The island-wide pattern, as an ideological graphic configuration, produces two or more interlocking space cells or geometric forms of relational lines. The patterns recur yet they are flexible and functional according to adherents of a faith or faiths. The forms, "pure" or otherwise, are realized in a certain context usually provoked by a need. We are dealing with a system of relationships or forms of status which change dynamically according to the realities of social change. Each belief system is a total system that transmits spiritual and functional meaning and value. Static meaning and function trivializes the belief system's significance and human use in the dynamic sense.

Therefore, I will proceed with the format Gananath Obeyesekere (1966:8–9) presented as a model of the Sinhalese Buddhist belief system from his Raṃbadeniya study. Here I will not deal with the specifics of Raṃbadeniya, but as Obeyesekere has done, I will expand to the Sinhalese belief system.[3] In this structure, the Buddha remains as the highest essence of moral goodness and supreme wisdom. The *text and context* of Sinhalese Buddhism differ, as everywhere in the Theravāda world; and the Buddha and his monks (*saṅgha*) are respected as the ideal form of human existence in terms of Buddhist philosophy and practice (Swearer 1981).

---

[3] In the quest for charting Buddhist or religious "cosmography" in Theravāda cultures see Ames 1961, 1966, Brohm 1963, Klausner 1964, Pfanner 1966, Spiro 1966, 1967, Tambiah 1970, Evers 1972, 1977, Reynolds 1976, Kirsch 1977, Seneviratne 1977, Southwold 1982, Keyes 1983, and Holt 1991.

The Buddhist monks are respected for their moral code which is based on the *Vinaya* which is a title of a text derived from the term *vinaya nīti*: "to lead away (from evil) to discipline" (de Silva 1980:148). Each member of the *saṅgha* must adhere to the code given in the strict *Pātimokkha* which contains 227 rules. The lay Buddhists usually respect and follow the first five of the ten precepts listed below. A novice (*sāmaṇera*) who is not a proper full fledged monk adheres to the full ten essential precepts.

(1) the precept to abstain from taking life
(2) the precept to abstain from taking what is not given
(3) the precept to abstain from wrong conduct in sexual desires
(4) the precept to abstain from telling lies
(5) the precept to abstain from intoxicating liquors which occasion heed-lessness
(6) the precept to abstain from eating at the wrong time
(7) the precept to abstain from seeing dancing, music vocal and instrumental, and shows
(8) the precept to abstain from high beds and big beds
(9) the precept to abstain from wearing garlands, perfumes and unguents, from finery and adornment
(10) the precept to abstain from accepting gold or silver

(Gombrich 1971:65–66)

Monks live together in a "pure good" intentional community of the proper attitude and education. Although, Gombrich (1971) and other scholars have shown that there is a difference between the way monks should act and their actual behavior, I would say that this is an observation of the "precept and practice" dyad that can be found in any tradition where people are expected to practice a discipline from an ideal code of ethics.

In the popular tradition, the Buddhist monks are respected by those who honor the entire network of traditional language, history, philosophy — shrines and temples — and just daily courtesies. Some city and town Sinhalese have grown up to display little respect to the tradition, therefore they disregard some monks as imperfect or free-loaders on the society. But, this negative view is the result of unfulfilled expectations concerning Sinhalese culture at large. If a person is denied traditional means of affluence (according to one's expectations) then the person faults tradition and family. Many suburban Sinhalese youths blame the "culture" for not advancing with the times. For them the society is pointed backward towards the roots of an ancient civilization which has long since ceased to provide any kind of viable livelihood. Monks are the symbols for the complete traditional network. If the tradition is devalued, then the *saṅgha* suffers. But in terms

of the Sinhalese at large, only a few individuals openly express displeasure
with the *saṅgha*. Certainly, most Sinhalese respect their traditional values
and give the impression that the monks are men to be revered. Monks are
honored as "venerable," and as "elder," when laymen are addressing them.
People who do not honor the monks usually remain silent. But, to return to
my point, the Buddha and his monks are praiseworthy for their existence.
Presently, very few monks aspire to, or are expected to reach, *buddhahood*
(*nibbāna*) in the immediate future (Maquet 1975a:14).

The next level as expressed by Gananath Obeyesekere (1966:9–12) and
other authors is the guardian deities just under the Buddha/*saṅgha* situation. In Śrī Laṅkā there are five paramount deities who protect the country under the Buddha's name: Saman, Vishnu, Kataragama (or Skandha),
Nātha, and Pattini; and also two others: Upulvan and Vibhīsana. These
deities grant favors or protect individuals and territories. Punishment only
comes to those persons who sin. This is the level of the *dēvāle*: the shrine
of the guardian deity. I studied at the Kataragama Dēvāle, Badulla, in the
Ūva Province. The *kapurālas* (priests of the deity shrine) made their living
performing daily rituals for a direct income. In a way, the *dēvāle* was a
place where people could relieve themselves emotionally of a problem by
placing their difficulties before the image of the deity. The real image was
placed in the secret sanctuary of the inner shrine where only the *kapurālas*
visited. A painted curtain of the youthful deity was placed in public view.
Kataragama represents the guardian deity of southern Śrī Laṅkā and the
powerful deity of war. This important deity is honored by Sinhalese and
Hindu Tamils alike who take the usual pilgrimage to the main shrine in the
Southern Province.

A third level of the pantheon is composed of a host of evil spirits (e.g.,
ghosts and "demons") who inhabit local village places such as graveyards,
crossroads, and abandoned huts. The spirits are evil and largely inferior
to the deities. They are considered "irrational" and cause senseless pain
to individuals without just cause. The people are usually afraid of such
spirits, which manifest themselves in specific physical and mental illnesses.
The illnesses are common and plentiful—and the cures usually require a
counter ritual of healing craft performed by an exorcist. The ceremonies
are many; yet each ritual is directed to the illness at hand. A relative of
an individual inflicted with a disease will employ exorcists whom give a
diagnosis of the affliction and order a dance performance. This exorcists'
ritual comes under the Buddhist purview as a form of compensation for the
pure philosophical form. It allows people to work out immediate suffering
with a professional who intervenes by use of spirits. The belief in spirits is
common in Śrī Laṅkā as well as in Southeast Asia. Spirits are an established

part of the Theravāda Buddhist popular pantheon since earliest times as they are depicted in Buddhist heritage stories.

The entire pantheon is a moral structural hierarchy divided into three or more sections, sub-sections, or gradations of participating good/evil forces. The simple structuring of the Sinhalese belief system is a method of illustrating a pattern or model for presentation based on the social facts.

In the subsequent sections, the reader will be guided by the permission of the three Sinhalese individuals who have dealt with their belief system as religious practitioners. Each adherent is a native of the Sinhalese rural society; yet working and living in variant dimensions.

The Sinhalese

The most concise and complete definition of the Sinhalese I have found, and which applies to this study, is from a note of explanation in *Sinhalese Monastic Architecture: The Vihāras of Anurādhapura* (1974:8–9) by Senake Bandaranayake:

> The terms *Sinhalese* and *Ceylonese* are sometimes, though not always, used here synonymously. There is, however, a distinction between them that is usually apparent in context, but which may require a brief explanation. *Ceylon* (Sinh. *Śrī Lankā*) and *Ceylonese* are the terms generally used today to refer in a comprehensive way to the geographical and national entity. The Ceylonese nation includes the two major linguistic and cultural groups, the Sinhalese and the Tamils, as well as other nationalities. On the other hand, the term *Sinhala*—which has possibly a clan or totemistic origin and from which is derived *Sinhalese*—was often used in historic times in the same sense as the modern [usage] *Ceylon* and *Ceylonese*—that is to say in both a geo-political and ethnological sense. Strictly speaking, *Sinhalese* is today a historical and a linguistic description which has cultural and ethnological and has been given racial connotations. The scientific use of this term in a cultural or ethnological sense is justified in so far as the Sinhalese-speaking people have a distinct historical existence and were the most numerous and prominent social and cultural group in Ceylon throughout its long history. This is not to imply, however, that the history of Ceylon is solely the history of a Sinhalese-speaking people, or that their culture is some pure, self-perpetuating and self-contained entity, without any connections or interrelations with Tamil-speaking or other elements. The racial use—i.e. in a physiological sense—of the term *Sinhalese*, not uncommon today, is not only insidious but, as far as we can see, has no real scientific basis. Thus, when we speak here of a *Sinhalese* tradition we mean in fact the dominant and distinctive indigenous cultural

traits of the island, without chauvinist or racist overtones. *Ceylonese,* on the other hand, is used to refer in a more general and comprehensive way to the cultural—or social, geographical, *etc.*—features, both indigenous and imported, which are to be found in the island of Ceylon. In current Ceylonese practice the form *Sinhala,* both as a noun and as an adjective, is preferred to *Sinhalese,* when writing in English or some other modern European language. In order to avoid confusion—largely of a grammatical nature—the original anglicisation *Sinhalese* is used throughout this study.

The Sinhalese are the majority people of Śrī Lankā: 74% of the people are Sinhalese and about 90% of those are Buddhists. The next largest group is known as Tamil (18.1%) who are divided between the 12.6% *Śrī Lankān* (i.e., Ceylon) Tamils of northern Jaffna, northeastern areas, and towns (including Colombo); and 5.5% classified as "Indian" Tamils who were employed by the British to attend to tea, coffee, and some rubber estates in the central highlands. Most Tamils are Hindus, but some are Christians. To arrive at the following figures, I consulted Maloney 1974a:157, *Śrī Lankā, Department of Census and Statistics 1981, UN Population Studies* 1986:293, *National Atlas of Śrī Lankā,* 1988:68-69, and Peacock 1989:18. Śrī Lankā figured 13.4 million people in 1973 with a rise by 1986 to 16.4 million and currently at press time had a population *estimated* at about 17.4 million. Adherents of faiths are in my opinion:

68.7% Theravāda Buddhists

15.4% Hindus, reduction in population due to out-of-country Tamils

7.6% Muslims (Islamic), population increasing

7.5% Christians (85% Roman Catholic)

0.8% other affiliations, including adherents of multiple faiths from the above (e.g., Buddhism), and Zoroastrianism (Parsees), Sufism, and beliefs among various individuals and groups such as the Vädda (Veddhas) and Chinese descendants

Śrī Lankā is a plural society divided along ethnic lines including religions, castes, languages, generations, and so on. The national model holds that Sinhalese are cultivators by tradition. Being Sinhalese usually implies being Theravāda Buddhist. Group classifications can be ambiguous when it comes to individuals. Generalizations apply to the groups—but the individuals are dispersed; the type (i.e., caste, "pure" type) becomes a relic or place holder for individual affinity to the group. Personal life style is chosen by feelings and national or group alternatives. So a cinnamon peeler who belongs to a specific caste (i.e., *salāgama*) might abandon or never know "traditional" occupation in reality—but continues to maintain caste affinity to some extent. The generalizations which define the group are felt to be only a line of secure attachment for necessary social requirements. The individual might remain in the caste as a cinnamon peeler, or choose an alternative life style, such as religious life in the monastery, a generalized laborer, or a scholarly existence.

In the history of Śrī Lankā or the Sinhalese Buddhist society, the reader must come to terms with an integrated plural system of beliefs and practices handed down and assimilated, and changed to various degrees to the present generation. As presented earlier, the structure Gananath Obeyesekere offers for the belief system illustrates a pyramid hierarchy existing at the ideal orthodox level and at the popular level. As an academic view, maintaining Buddhism in "purity" would not match the view and objective of a people who have different life styles: farming, trading, or crafting-items for a living. The absolute pursuit of a religious life has been the way of a few individuals who were known as forest-dwelling monks (*arañña-vāsī bhikkhu*) and the village monks (*grāma-vāsī bhikkhu*). They are usually educated in the ways of the Buddha at the philosophical level. On the so-called mundane level, the people (laymen or householders) practice a complex of religious beliefs that are of Hindu, Buddhist, Islamic, or indigenous origin.

In accordance with the syncretic nature of the South Asian belief systems, adherents of particular faiths will also reach past their religious label and associate in some way with the beliefs and deities of "separate systems." The belief systems are integrated by national feeling on a need basis. According to the Sinhalese, the Buddha and "pure" Buddhist practices remain paramount to Buddhist adherents and the "Hindu" deities or "local" spirits are utilized when there is a need for them in some crisis situation or a desire to make use of all the spiritual options. The use of available alternatives, spiritual or otherwise, is a South Asian way of doing things. Everyday weaker deities are rising and stronger ones are falling. Of course, in usual research the major deities and faiths are studied, because they are seen as the most visibly important to be known. About three hundred years after the Buddha was enlightened, Buddhism was one of the contending faiths in South Asia, and Emperor Aśoka made Buddhism the state religion of the largest empire in South Asia. Then, more than a thousand years later, Buddhism declined and essentially perished from South Asia except for some strongholds in Bengal, Tibet, and Śrī Lankā.

In the same manner, the deities of South Asia have risen and fallen in name, image, and strength. The favorable deities in Śrī Lankā today were not the most powerful ones just a few generations ago. Three hundred years ago, the deity cults in Śrī Lankā were relatively more popular than orthodox Buddhism. The deities remain powerful in a certain sense as they are manifest in temples and shrines; and, they receive large offerings and public participation at their events and ceremonies.

Each deity (like the Buddha) has a specific life account and source of power. Presently, as a protector of Lankā, Kataragama is the most popular deity, following the Buddha. Kataragama has his territory in the Southern Province, (south of the Kalutara River) in the area where "Sinhalese culture" shifted after set-backs by European powers. The Portuguese destroyed the temple at Dondra for Upulvan Deviyo along the southern coast. The old Kandyan patron deity Nātha soon lost importance after the Kandyan Kingdom (1597–1815) collapsed as a Sinhalese independent state and came under British administration. So, for about 450 years Kataragama has been rising in importance. It is interesting to mention that already in the early 1800s, when the Sinhalese generals were trying to hold their defences in Ūva Province, Kataragama was established, as the deity of greatest importance for the reestablishment of the Sinhalese kingdom. The Kataragama Dēvāle in Badulla, Ūva Province, was consecrated by the generals as a place of great sanctity for a powerful revival. In the Kandy Convention of 1815, the British provided *Article Five* for the protection of temples and *dēvāles* to continue valuable Sinhalese rituals in order to stabilize the situation (Ven. Ratanasara 1972:40).

*   *   *

In Śrī Lankā, the belief system boundaries are usually set by academics, but at the popular level those lines are crossed according to daily life. Common frustration causes the individual to turn slightly or radically in some other direction, in or out of the prescribed tradition. I view the belief system in Śrī Lankā to offer serviceable activities for "worship and therapy" (Ames 1963:46). Michael Ames (1963) suggests that in Śrī Lankā, Buddhism and what he calls "magical-animism" have remained distinct features, though complementary to the more overall religious system. The dimensions act through the respective functions: first, worship and, second, therapy. "Buddhism is concerned with sin, rebirth, and the fate of the soul; magical-animism is solely concerned with well-being in this life itself" (*ibid.*; see also for discussion, R. N. Bellah, *Some Suggestions for the Systematic Study of Religion*, ms., Harvard University mentioned in the Ames' article). The "worship and therapy sub-systems" create a problem for me as I observe them to be features operational in all of the dimensions of the Śrī Lankā belief systems. Gananath Obeyesekere's presentation in *Medusa's Hair* (1981) and his *The Cult of the Goddess Pattini* (1984) are ideal case studies for the understanding of the separate and yet multi-dimensional qualities of the religious practices in Śrī Lankā. Certainly Hindus are different from Buddhists, but the belief systems are usually more conciliatory than conflicting, both at the popular centers, such as Kataragama as well as at the academic level. In the prevailing cultural system, the belief system is a pathway for the realization of a destiny in terms of livelihood, career, and health. The participants in the system operate along balancing health practices and different elemental forces (spiritual and physical) to achieve human ends.

Life Account

Anthropological data of all kinds are difficult to obtain and are often of questionable reliability and validity, but they are all fundamentally biographical.

—L. L. Langness 1965:53.

Account. A narrative relation of events in a life, or lives; frequently used in titles before the word *biography* was in general use; an *account* implies a methodical treatment of a life...

—Nicholas Rowe
(Winslow 1980:1)

A life account is a condensed graphic life or a portrait of a life recorded to show the individual's cultural role by an ethnographer or a person involved in the life/psychological human sciences. I will use the term life account as the sequential process of the cultural life recorded to display the individual in social context. That is to say a life account is a series of portraits at different life-ages and social-cycles similar to the "snapshots" in a photograph album. The anthropologist does the task of interviewing and arranging the life sequences into ordered reflections. This *summoned* life history is made to see how the individual lives within a tradition. The life account or life history explores a social role (Ruby 1977).

Human Image

Myth *is* the instant vision of a complex process that ordinarily extends over a long period.

—Marshal MacLuhan 1964:38.

The human image *changes* in time and in space in each culture. It seems that each age and culture produces an image of the human form which differs. In the painting and literature of peoples there are self-evaluations and in-depth psychological views. The craft of writing reflects the psychology of the author's mind and ethos. In contemporary Western literature, "beginning with James Joyce's *Ulysses*," the process of writing has become, first, multi-dimensional—e.g., the portrayal of the same individual or event though the eyes of different protagonists or moods of the same protagonist (Rosenthal 1971:3); second, introspective for the act of knowing the self to demonstrate to others (e.g., cross-cultural psychic unity understanding); and third, culture context centered the awareness of the parameters of a person's ethos or *zeitgeist*.

43

In each cultural age, there is a way to express the individual nature: first, in a classical way, as in the hymns and verses of the epic human, and second, in the idiosyncratic approach of the *real* person. But, in every case, the person is a social-being with a story coming through a writer.[1]

In the study of anthropological life histories, each individual becomes the vantage point for the social ethos (see Shostak 1983, Crapanzano 1984, Denzin 1989, Ryder 1992, and Gullestad 1993). In this sense, the life becomes a "social horizon" of certain relationships which encompass a network of people (Maquet 1971:9). And the anthropologist records the view of the individual's interpretation of his, or her, interactive social negotiations. This is a reflective process for both the individual participant and the anthropologist. A working literature is available in anthropology for the study of life histories. *Lives: An Anthropological Approach to Biography* by L. L. Langness and Gelya Frank (1981) is an excellent reference for the study of ethno-biographies in respects to method, validity, and presentational style.

I will speak of a few important writings. Vincent Crapanzano wrote "The Life History in Anthropological Field Work" (1977) to express the difficulties involved with an informant who related his fanciful experiences about himself and others. Crapanzano stated that, as an anthropologist, he had difficulty with his own objectivity in a life account case study. He writes of his informant:

> There was always something captivating about Tuhami's discourse. It was as though he wanted to entrap me, to enslave me in an intricate web of fantasy and reality...I became an articulatory pivot about which he would spin out his fantasies...I was, so to speak, created to create him...(*ibid.*:6).

Crapanzano continues by saying that his eventual writing about this Moroccan individual, Tuhami, according to his own "questions, expectations, musings, and theoretical confabulations," was a portrait akin to himself (*ibid.*).

Akemi Kikumura recalls from her research concerning the life history of her family through her mother's account:

> The recollection of past events inevitably led to the problems that faced the participant in the present, and those past events were discussed in terms of causes for the participant's present situation (Kikumura 1981:147).

---

[1] Concerning terminology and bibliography used in life accounts, Donald J. Winslow (1980) has edited *Life-Writing: Glossary of Terms in Biography, Autobiography, and Related Forms.*

Akemi Kikumura also related that "I have found that the kind of data collected from the participant is strongly affected by the events that occur prior to the interview" (*ibid.*). This referred to dilemma is really unavoidable, as individuals can not be separated from the research process of the life account. John J. Honigmann wrote a very provocative article called "The Personal Approach in Cultural Anthropological Research" to consider and defend the human-sense in anthropological research. The suggested approach draws on the investigator's *sensitivity, depth of thought, speculative ability, speculative freedom, imagination, intuition,* and *intellectual flexibility* for a humanistic attention to creative work.

> In addition tö employing sensitivity. . .every person using the personal approach brings to bear on his/her work a unique biographical background and configuration of personal interests and values, not all of which are fully conscious. . .(Honigmann 1976:244).

The personal approach means self-awareness to the process of research as creative. Just as a dramatist communicates a message by placing individual experiences into the aesthetic form of a performance, the life account writer composes by cultural design and the key stages of the participant's life.

Daisaku Ikeda wrote in the preface to his English edition of the *Living Buddha: An Interpretive Biography*:

> It is my firm conviction that one can seek to discover and understand another human individual only through the medium of one's own identity as a human being. . .In this respect my portrait of him. . .is no doubt strongly colored by the image that I have formed in my mind of him as the leader of a religious organization (1976:viii).

"The Study of Life History: Gandhi" written by David G. Mandelbaum, 1973, is a contemporary work to explore the composition of a life. He chose the life of Mohandas Karamchand Gandhi within key *frames of experience* (dimensions) which were connected to a person's eventful life. The life frames were called *turnings* which occurred when a "newness" of life was accomplished. The person adapted to change within a psychological continuum of life. In this way, (*Mahātma*) Mohandas Gandhi's life history was ordered by Mandelbaum and studied as a kind of aesthetic arrangement of the life manifest in dimensions, turnings, and subsequent changes.

David G. Mandelbaum (1973) also made a distinction between what he called life passage studies and life history studies: life passage or life cycle studies ". . .emphasize the requirements of society, showing how the people of a group socialize and enculturate their young in order to make them into viable members of society"; and ". . .life history studies, in contrast emphasize the experiences and requirements of the individual—how the person copes with society rather than how society copes with the stream of individuals" (*ibid.*:177).

Also Erik H. Erikson (1975) dealt with the life of Gandhi in terms of his dimensions of "identity crisis" in the *disciplined subjectivity* of investigating the following life stages: first, "personal sameness and continuity" as a shared world image of self; second, "a state of being and becoming" (self identity and growing up; third, *developmental period* as in *adolescence* and *youth* which include the "*psychobiological* factors which secure the somatic basis for a coherent sense of vital selfhood"...and the *psychological* factors which "can prolong the crisis (painfully, but not necessarily unduly) where a person's idiosyncratic gifts demand a prolonged *search* for a corresponding ideological and occupational setting, or where historical change forces a postponement of adult commitment"; and fourth, a dependence on the *past*. The *historical past* gives the individual "the resource of strong identifications made in childhood, while it relies on new models encountered in youth, and depends for its conclusion on workable roles offered in young adulthood...[which] contribute to its preservation and renewal" (*ibid.*:18–19). His point is that stages are identifiable in the life history which assist in the analysis of the person's present socio-psychology.

The *knowing* of another person is a mental process. The presentation of an individual is an art. The dramatic multi-dimensional approach is found in *The Woman Warrior: Memories of a Girlhood Among Ghosts* (the dream novel of a Chinese American growing-up on different planes of consciousness) by Maxine Hong Kingston (1977) and the introspective biography like the journalistic novel *Nausea* (existentialist fiction) by Jean-Paul Sartre (1964). These books present the person in idiosyncratic time. Other writings center on the meaning of the multi-dimensional person. In Ralph Ruddock's "Conditions of Personal Identity" (1972), the life is approached from six components: self, identity, personality, role, perspective, and project. Here the "self knowing" depends on a relationship of the listed components in the context of *self* and *society*.

Gelya Frank's article "Finding the Common Denominator: A Phenomenological Critique of Life History Method," (1979) states that in terms of humanness: "Many researchers are now consciously drawing on their own selves through autobiographical writing...opening insights into the process..." which produces the life history construct unavailable to outward looking, listening, and recording (*ibid.*:89).

Once the individual has a separate identity within the frame of social reality, or group type, the individual can use himself, or herself, as a natural hue in the spectrum of culture. The known self can then explore toward the reaches of any mutual relationship. As the mind increases its capacity to enter intentional relationships, the physical body follows in a natural way.

A Life History Writer

In striving to become part of the whole, there is nevertheless a greater belief in the relatedness of all people, in the hope that one day all will be joined in the brotherhood of humanity.

—Stanley L. M. Fong 1973:126

The state of *being:* is one of actualized life. A "life history is a text" of the life as observed and presented by the life history writer (Langness and Frank 1981). The picture presented in the life history is created as a *social fact.* The life history writer "grasps" those cognized experiences expressed by the informant (other person) and writes them as a "sober description" (Schutz 1967) or "thick description" (Geertz 1973) including aesthetic quality for literary merit.[2]

In entering the role of a life history writer, I thought about the effect of my own influence in the task of gathering the material. The task is based on a relationship of mutual friendship. The understanding of one another is essential for a common trust/companionship.

The world is a relationship. The person... "understands the world by interpreting his own lived experiences of it, whether these experiences be of inanimate things, of animals, or of his fellow human beings..." (Schutz 1967:108). A key research premise is that when one studies another person, there is a mutual humanness, a basis in the understanding. The quality in the human sciences is beyond statistics and samples. Theodore Abel stated that "...Vico acclaimed mathematics and human history as subjects about which we have a special kind of knowledge ... created by us" (Abel 1948:211). In or out of society, each person develops a cultural/natural relationship; "...solitary man [as the hermit lives in isolation] has at least the company of his operating procedures" (Berger and Luckmann 1967:53). Relationships are intrinsic to the nature of life. And for the relationship to be meaningful, there must be a direct consciousness for the pattern of

---

[2] Clifford Geertz borrowed the notion of "thick description" from Gilbert Ryle. The "thick description" interprets the thing or events in the World as meaningful to say what is a "twitch" of the eye or a "wink." As the "wink" communicates a message, it is done, "first, deliberately, second, to someone in particular, third, to impart a particular message, fourth, according to a socially established code, and fifth, without cognizance of the rest of the company" (Geertz 1973:6). Thus, a "twitch" of the eye is defined as a contraction of the eyelid, and not a gesture.

the relationship. The achievement of understanding a relationship gives a pattern to common reality. Our own culture is our common maintenance system. Humanness is a common reality. A world of natural energy and forces, emotions and feelings are the ties to any face-to-face relationship. Institutions in that way are external to personal understanding: "The individual cannot understand them by introspection" (*ibid.*:60). "As the individual reflects about the successive movements of his experience, he tries to fit their meanings into a consistent biographical framework" (*ibid.*:64).[3]

The concept of *verstehen* stems from the European enlightenment (e.g., Comte) which re-discovered the Greek motto "know thy self." Self knowledge is an aspect of human knowledge. Authors or writers of novels use *verstehen* as a standard to "know" others in their work. In ethnography, the researcher uses himself, or herself, as a basic resource in the endeavor to observe and interpret human action. Anthropology is a discipline where a person uses empathetic knowledge to investigate human manifestations. "*Verstehen* gives. . .the certainty that a given interpretation of behavior is a possible one" (*ibid.*:213). Mutual humanness is only a factor in determining behavior. Factors must come into play and be systematized as evidence. In order to track evidence, different procedures are used (e.g., direct observations, measures, statistics, the charting of social systems).

The act of the human interpersonal relationship is a symmetrical performance of sharing events, feelings, spaces, and knowledge for the future. The stories come from the questions people ask about each other. The answers come in spontaneous meanings which emerge from degrees of honesty and distortion.

I will give a guide for what I think the mutual relationship should be, in terms of intention, for the life history writer and participants:

(1) The intention of the life history writer is to be *intelligible* to everyone concerned. (Usually a written statement of method and use of the material should be accessible and in a language for anyone to read).

(2) The *relationship* must be open and honest.

(3) *Humility* and *faithfulness* are essential traits for the life history writer

---

[3] Apart from anthropological sources, Jay Ruby (1988) mentioned that there is a trend of "reflexive, films made by artists, documentarians" and others belonging to a "tradition of autobiographical, self-portrait, [and] family" in the spirit of "self representation" and biographical areas which I do not touch upon, including *avant garde* American or French materials. A source given by Ruby is by John Katz, *Autobiography: Film/Video/Photograph* (1987), an exhibition catalog published by the Art Gallery of Ontario, Canada. Also see the work of Wendy Ewald.

to establish and maintain the trust and integrity for everyone involved.

(4) Careful *attention* must be paid to the entire affair, including the act of tuning-in to the nuances of the flowing life.

(5) The writer must live up to the charter or *commitment* to the individuals involved in the life history writing process.

During the dialogue of the life history conversation, there is a sense of *growing old together*. The unfolding of some key remembered experiences becomes shared experience. Perhaps the dialogue becomes misinterpreted, but it is ours. Our "context" and "choice" for the life history is our own sharing. And, in the act, there is self definition.

Every point mentioned deals with the ethics of the life history as a human process. The life history writer must search conscience for the most factual image. In terms of quality, each constellation of moods and thoughts should be placed under an intentional gaze for aesthetic composition. The life history should represent the re-affirmation of the personal life as experienced or imagined by the informant. The life history writer must use personal skill to recognize patterns and show them.

The Individual

A thinking human being is an adaptive system; his goals define the interface between his inner and outer environments.

—Herbert Alexander Simon 1969:25

It is my premise from Herbert Alexander Simon that human behavior is effectively adaptive and directed toward a set of cultural goals.[4] The manifestation of those behaviors is largely reflected in the outer environment. Only a few limited gestures are revealed "of the physiological machinery that enables him [or her] to think" (Simon 1969:26). The social and natural environment determine the artificial nature of the self. It is an act of *interface*: human interior and the social or natural environment. The apparent complexity of the person's behavior is largely dependent on the personal quest in terms of goals conditioned by an environmental/cultural system as Price-Williams states:

Each individual culture adapts to the specific demands of its environment, which through the culture's social system leads to the development of particular psychological skills required for survival (1975:20).

---

[4] In the anthropological literature this emphasis comes from the "individual and culture" — Goldenweiser 1923, Kardiner 1939, Kluckhohn 1949, Harring 1956, Hsu 1961 and 1972, Singer 1961, Barnouw 1963, Williams 1975, Langness and Frank 1981, Spiro 1987, Geertz 1988, Goldschmidt 1990, and Obeyesekere 1990.

As I am interested in specific case studies of living individuals and the literature concerning the image of the South Asian self, as prompted by the anthology *Self and Biography: Essays on the Individual and Society in Asia*, Wang Gungwu, ed., which "...could more directly be approached through the fields of literature and history..." (1975:1).

> In South Asia, the Hindu-Buddhist tradition acknowledged the impor-
> tance of Self by seeking to check its aggrandizement and by limiting
> its place in this world at any particular time. Knowing except whether
> they might show a capacity to merge with the universal, with the infi-
> nite and the eternal (*ibid.*:2).

In the literature of the Buddha and the various other *sages* demonstrates the South Asian trait of strength in self knowing in writing. As Wang Gungwu wrote in his introduction "There was...no meaningful biography [in South Asia] except where it might demonstrate how a few extraordinary men conquered their selves" (*ibid.*).

Written accounts of kings, noblemen, and important historical people are given in old manuscripts and recently published "memoirs" of families such as the Bandaranaikes (Gooneratne 1986). During the 20th Century, with ethno-religious revivals, many historic works have been reprinted by Buddhist organizations, scholars, and the government press of Śrī Lankā. One such manuscript, *Rāsinha Hāmuduruvannē Rājanitiya*, gives the activities and accomplishments of King Rājasinha II tracing his life of politics (Ven. Wachissara 1961:12). The salient feature life accounts which I have chosen operate in this vein of South Asian writings. *They are accounts of men, important to a belief system, who share model title and positions of moral responsibility, yet they are life accounts that are seldom written unless an ethnographer or social scientist becomes interested in the case study of the individual.* Each participant recorded is a village man who represents a source of local strength for Sinhalese rural society, with a special task in the unity of the social belief system.

*   *   *

There has been a literary heritage of life history accounts in South Asian traditions stemming from the *Avadānas*, and other works including *Nalopākhyāna* (see Malaviya 1958), *Buddha Carita* (see Johnston 1978), and *Kādambarī* (Kale 1924, Samarasinghe 1957). Sinhala and Pāli literature are rich with legendary accounts of the Buddhist lay individual who is involved with the events at various levels in the lives of *dēvatās*, sages, and kings (Reynolds 1970). In these writings, biographical material could be found intertwined in mythology (R. Obeyesckere and Fernando 1981). Historically, Emperor Aśoka has been represented in edicts with commentary on his accomplishments from the 3rd Century B.C. Remaining evidence in South Asia displays historical life in stone, brick, and plaster (Loofs 1975:28) from writings and given oral accounts.

Sinhalese Aesthetics

When nations grow old
The arts grow cold,
And commerce settles on every tree.

—William Blake
(Coomaraswamy 1956:vi)

Sahaja, sahaja, everyone speaks of *sahaja,*
But who knows what *sahaja* means?

—Chaṇḍidas
(Coomaraswamy 1971:127)

As an ideational system to understand the balance, form, and texture of the data, Sinhalese aesthetics influenced the research and the outcome. The data was ordered and presented according to the aesthetic system of the culture. Here, I discuss the aesthetic influences.

In the world at large, there is the human vision of aesthetics;[1] a mountain standing among clouds is beautiful (it is natural to consider). Then, there is art: an abstract representation of a world fragment represented by culture. The natural mountain is expressed on canvas according to the vision of the artist who applies line, shape, shade, form, perspective, and color within a *human context* vis-a-vis a natural environment to create illusion and emotion. There is really no mountain on the canvas, only the image of one. If the image is successfully painted and seen, it will hold the observer's attention. The human attention is drawn to rest—as in the human pleasure of seeing the original mountain scene. A state of contemplation is entered; the discursive life dissolves in a murmur—the sound of flowing rapids in the distance.

The anatomy of art is established and searched for in each society to represent life force. Thought is present from the structure of an art form to its material and craft qualities; but how it comes out is the result of many factors. The artist presents work as a framed abstract of the world. To have readable art, the presented abstract requires the imagination and skill of the artist. In the ultimate sense, art is the artificial vehicle for the human spirit.

---

[1] See Masaharu Anesaki (1915) *Buddhist Art in its Relation to Buddhist Ideal, with Special Reference to Buddhism in Japan*; and Clifford Geertz (1976) "Art as a Cultural System."

Images: Buddha and Śiva

In the Sinhalese case, the image of the historic Buddha is refined and stable in a sense of peace within a dynamic and sometimes chaotic world of spirits. The Buddha is a *maṇḍala* form which is etched in red under layers of semi-transparent pigment. The halo or flame on the Buddha's head lifts the image in celestial lightness. Floating in the middle, yet grounded with stability of magnificence, the Buddha radiates a presentational self to the observer. In a similar way, the dancing Śiva, in the South Indian tradition, is lightly dancing in the space of circle of flames: the fire-points of *desire*. Within the context of the flames, the image is seen with a central focus. Śiva is the mighty and powerful, or the destroyer, in the graphic dance of gesture and grace (see Jouveau-Dubreuil 1937).

Śiva is seen as a dynamic force in a serious aspect, to be awed and respected as the image of discipline. On the other hand, the deity is humorous as he dances in space with one foot on a dwarf of ignorance. In a third view, Śiva gives the essence of calm in an effortless pose. Like the Buddha, Śiva gives something special to the meaning of life altered from the natural existence. This is the window for the imagination in which the viewer can enter. In the aesthetic sense the vision remains constant: the supreme contemplation of image. The visual difference comes in ideological form: the Buddha is soft and subtle in the curves of his body: compassionate. Śiva is angular and reaching with dynamic body-limbs. The images represent different paradigms in Buddhist and Hindu art structure. Yet, the aesthetic essence is matched to a simple South Asian aesthetic purpose. Once the purpose is understood in the ultimate sense, then nothing in the art is strange. The forms and shapes are rational. In the frame of the design, the viewer rests in contemplation to see the aesthetic composition. The illusion is complete in the fabric of the bodies, which show no strain or muscle as the deities act with ease. As the themes stem from South Asian traditions generally, the viewer rests in the comfort of a similar value system, yet the Buddhist and Hindu are basically different in the sense that they are placed in two categories, not only for religious name sake, but because the belief systems manifest basic cultural identities.

The Buddhist tradition of art design emphasizes *samādhi*, which has slightly softened the Hindu themes so the image of Śiva is more humorous and milder in the Sinhalese version. The transformation is always taking place, as in the Southeast Asian Cambodia example of Hindu art being adapted by the Khmer artists for Khmer tastes. The choices are usually open to the artist within the context of acceptable norms.

The artist or craftsman experiments with kinds of values until the qualities are achieved to make whatever object constructed is aesthetic. To a degree, this process works toward a living aesthetic, as in the life accounts of the men of this study.[2]

Aesthetic Determinants

Art is now one of the strongest evidences of the basic unity of mankind.

—Meyer Schapiro 1953:291

Jacques Maquet (1979) follows a grammar of aesthetics which is based on indigenous culture.[3] This system is shaped by the available choices of values and available materials (resources). In the Sinhalese world, the aesthetic system comes from an enduring South Asian tradition which is the key to formal and popular notions of what should be—what is correct or beautiful. The feelings associated with a cultural aesthetic could be seen as a *bias* or way of *seeing* within a particular tradition. Perhaps only the specialist of the aesthetics or tradition really sees the layers of meaning associated with art. This talent is cultivated by cultural and art specialists who can use their education and training for the purpose of gaining aesthetic knowledge. The specialist helps interpret art by setting reference standards on several levels. Artifacts or aesthetic objects have first, a network of experts who deal in the cultural art context; second, a particular context—within a tradition (indigenous setting), or outside the

---

[2] In contrast to the artists of this research, Herbert Read (1976:1) states that a Western rational public had little use for the eccentric few:

> EVER SINCE DEMOCRACY became a clear political conception in the city-state of Athens, democratic philosophers have been faced with the anomaly of the artist. It has seemed to them that the artist, by his very nature, cannot be accommodated within the structure of an egalitarian community. He is inevitably a social misfit, to normal people a psychotic, and for rational thinkers like Plato the only solution was to banish him from the community. A modern rationalist would probably recommend that he should be cured of his psychosis.

There are two main problems: (I) What is it that seems to *separate* the artist from the rest of the community, making him [or her] unique...[in society]? (2) What is it that nevertheless *reconciles* the community to this separatist individual—that is to say, what values does the artist contribute to the community that make the community accept or tolerate his [or her] presence among them?

[3] For anthropological distinction of "folk/court" art compared to "subsistence/production" methods and styles according to research, value, and utilization, see Jacques Maquet's *Aesthetic Anthropology*.

original tradition as a place where the aesthetic forms were not originally intended (e.g., a Buddha statue in a museum or gallery); and, third, the shape and form of the aesthetic object (see Maquet 1979, 1986).

Traditional forms are a model of ideal reality, or a model of quality. The aesthetic expression is in the content of Sinhalese art. As the Sinhalese say, the world is a reality (or just the way it is) and a person abstracts from it in order to make judgement, saying or manifestation. Art is the statement; it is understood through an individual's basic senses.[4] The individual artist really emerges after a struggle to learn: first, the technique of the art as a science; second, how to use intuition and feelings to transmit seemingly natural energy into the construction of art; and third, how to make a statement using the shape of the motif and symbol in color and form (Dufrenne 1973).

The aesthetic quality should be the essence of sharing human information with a concise point (symbol message). The aesthetic focus creates the artificial "we-ness": art purpose and art viewer. The entire relationship becomes an ethos experience: first, *space*; second, *time*; third, *other and myself happening*; fourth, *sense data*; and, fifth, *aesthetic feeling*. This notion of aesthetic quality influenced my procedure and shaped the process of ethnography. My research was based on the knowledge of aesthetics which I acquired while living in the Sinhalese monastery, and then at the other places of study including the university in Śrī Lankā.

The aesthetic qualifications for art works are observed as tastes or sentiments known as *rasa* offering (1) *śṛṅgāra*: love, (2) *karuṇā*: sympathy, (3) *vīra*: heroism, (4) *adbhūta*: wonder, (5) *hāsya*: mirth, (6) *bhayānaka*:

---

[4] Sinhalese Buddhist sense perception (Pāli, *saññā-kkhandha*) is divided into six areas: form, sound, odour, taste, bodily impression, and mental impression (Ven. Nyanatiloka 1972:86).

For further studies in "traditional perception" see Sarathchandra (1958) *Buddhist Psychology of Perception*, and Raniero Gnoli (1968) *The Aesthetic Experience According to Abhinavagupta* for classical South Asian works.

A sample of Sinhalese art studies include Paranavitana 1954, Coomaraswamy 1956, Wickramasinghe 1972, and von Schroeder 1992; for art approaches and concepts: Huxley 1954, Merriam 1964, Elsen 1967, Hospers 1969, Ortega y Gasset 1972, Martin 1972, Dufrenne 1973, Bettelheim 1976, Geertz 1976, Dexereux 1977, Greenholgh and Megaw 1978, Maquet 1979 and 1986, and Schechner 1990.

In the visual sense of Sinhalese temple art see renditions of traditional illustrations by artist Manjusri, and artist/architect L. K. Karunaratne (drawings in Paranavitana 1967).

terror, (7) *bībhatsa*: disgust, (8) *raudra*: wrath (anger or fury) which are the eight tastes (*aṭṭha rasa*); continuing with (9) *śānta*: sentiment of peace or sublime tranquillity, along with the eight, known as *nava rasa*, and (10) *vātsalya*: paternal fondness. These traits are expressed in dance, drumming, and poetry, and other art forms (see Coomaraswamy 1971).

The various tastes are employed because one is not enough to be trusted. Multi-dimentional levels of input are necessary for a *genuine* judgement to occur in terms of the material. Aesthetic considerations make for a clearer perspective. The key in aesthetic interpretation is open and disciplined awareness of the human senses when taking in the information at hand.

A book or a motion picture provides limited levels of sense bearing data. The reader or observer must utilize other resources from their own experience to complement and add-to the information given.

Linear Order. Chronological order is the method of compiling Sinhala Buddhist history. Gananath Obeyesekere pointed out to me that in relation to time this kind of Buddhist linear order is different from the Hindu multi-dimensional attitude of expression.

Meaningful Story Frames. Temple paintings are framed stories. The picture usually represents a single event or a sequence of events within a frame of the temple wall. The framed event allows the viewer to contemplate the picture for a particular message in the story.

Basic Colors. Sinhalese Buddhist painting is usually given to colors like saffron, red, sepia, and umber. Blue and green are used for contrasting impact for sky, ocean, river, or divinity sometimes in human shape.

Even-lighting. The aesthetic use of even-light in a painted scene gives a sense of soft and divine quality seeming to shelter the form from the sun by a canopy of sky. This divine shadowless-style is the technique used in most temple painting (see Bandaranayake and Jayasinghe 1986).

Narrative Story. The art of story telling revolves around the life of the Buddha. The story is told in the narrative fashion, a poem (*kavi*) or a Buddha Birth Story (*Jātaka*).

During the research, the Sinhalese aesthetic value became a key consideration. The aesthetic value system served as a basis for understanding the culture (see Geertz 1976, Dissanayake 1989, and Schechner 1990).

Ethnographic Time Concepts

The concept of time is critical in the understanding of the human life. The time duration process has conceptual organizational dimensions. Clifford Geertz (1966) proposed that the Balinese have two kinds of time concepts: ritual time or the "ritualized" past history which is stable (denies age sequence); and non-ritualized time which is pragmatic and mundane in the normal sense of daily activities (e.g., human aging). Arjun Appadurai (1981) offers still a third dimension, which he calls the cultural relative form, which has four categories—first, *authority*: cultural consensus for credibility of the past; second, *continuity*: cultural consensus as to the kinds of connections linking the past; third, *depth*: cultural consensus to variations of "time-depths" at differing levels; and fourth, *interdependence*: convention inter-relating other 'pasts' with the past. "Substantive conventions concerning each of these dimensions can, of course, vary both cross-culturally and intra-culturally" (*ibid.*:203). Thus, offered are different aspects of the orientation of the past: *ritual* (e.g., mythical), *pragmatic* or *mundane* (e.g., daily life), and *cultural interpretative* format. According to Appadurai, the cultural format sets a culture specific interpretation in motion. This concept is multi-dimensional to a common area (*ibid.*). In South Asia there is a continuum of literati civilization for the past two millennia, where groups have used written social charters (see Goody 1977). There also exist entire groups, such as the Veddās who conduct themselves by the charter of mythic time from memory. In the Hindu group, the notion of a mythic past (or timeless existence) prevails more strongly than in the Buddhist community where a stronger historical lineal tradition is the standard (Obeyesekere 1979). The two kinds of time-concepts exist in each other as there is an overlap of "time traditions." The standard (or charter) organization of time is a tendency for the individuals of a society to live by. But, the actual elements of the charter are multi-dimensional and individuals or groups could very well splinter-off "to live by" another tendency of time and start or continue by the rules of one or several "original" elements. The social charter of time is really an overall configuration of concepts emphasizing mental attitude and correct behavior.

The Sinhalese Buddhist Concept of Historic Time Duration

In the Sinhalese Buddhist tradition, the past, the ancient text, the notion of linear forward progression (even if modeled in an up-ward spiral), and the Anurādhapura image of the Buddha in *samādhi* are highly valued; but also respected are the images personified in the spontaneous poet, the modern artist, an internationally acknowledged political leader and so on. The present is valued as authority, if the past is included in the design.

Major literary traditions hold a charter for Sinhalese people. One is the historical writings of the *Mahāvamsa*, which traces the events of the Sinhalese Buddhist people since the origin of their civilization about twenty-five centuries ago. The text was written and continued in a linear sequence and the emphasis was placed on the key events of the monarchy. In this respect the historical work tends to be a secular document similar to the later royal *vamsa* or illustrated manuscripts of the Persian and Northwest South Asian kings. Another literary tradition is the corpus of Buddhist texts about the lives and beliefs of the Buddha. These writings came originally from Pāli and then later they were translated into Sinhala.

Like the historic writings of the *Mahāvamsa*, scholars established literary textual treaties on the Buddhist teachings based on the life of the Buddha—but the *Birth Stories (Jātaka)* which are of his lives and the consequential teachings, do not give an absolute sense of time duration (Rhys Davids 1880). The stories are timeless, ritualized, and mythical. Yet, the stories have time frame sequences and openness for interpretation.

Numerous are the monastic *Vinaya* (the rules given by the Buddha for the correct behavior of monks) or treaties for body and mind discipline by adherents of the Buddha/*dhamma*/*sangha* (triple gem). The treaties with commentaries or collection of sayings are ageless philosophical writings not confined to rituals (which could be said to have a limited time duration). This "highest textual" corpus makes full circle in a South Asian tradition because linear values of the *Mahāvamsa* style of writings are transcended to achieve multi-dimensional thought: philosophical awareness. The task and skill of writing stories tends to attach a beginning, middle, and end to a concept. The writing of the *Mahāvamsa* put the philosophy and events of a people into a linear history; the Buddha stories arrange a time duration in a lesser historic way using metaphor and altered time duration. In South Asia, written compilation of Buddhist thoughts, and sayings of religious men and women, are open to the oral tradition of philosophy and spontaneity, yet they were well organized teachings (see Ramanujan 1973).

In Sinhalese Buddhist tradition, a man on a public bus composes and recites poems using the cultural format, yet he is spontaneous. A family attends a temple service where the monks recite ancient *gāthā* (verse) from the original words of the great sage remaining on the *ola* leaves for centuries. In every case, the tradition retains the elements of first, "ritual/mythic" and second, "non-ritualistic" approach. On another plane is the third, cultural pattern or charter which produces socialization. The fourth, and final level, is a spontaneous or idiosyncratic style of the tradition or what is called "human" forces or individual characteristics. Altogether, the four part configuration composes a quality mental regime for living. When time is composed as art by an artist or craftsman in society, the result is an expression of ritual/non-ritual and traditional/spontaneous: aspects of aesthetic awareness. The skill of the artist or craftsman determines the tendency of the society to understand and accept or not-understand aesthetic behavior. The Sinhalese concept of time continuum is very basic to the entire thought structure of the social organization.

Life Account and Motion Picture

> ...an anthropologist who goes out to observe a society naturally produces what is called a synchronic study in which the society, including its religion, has its picture taken at one moment and is thus presented as if static.
>
> —Richard Gombrich 1971:3

As the life account or life history is an aesthetic composition, motion picture is also employed to include an audio/visual dimension. Margaret Mead wrote "The Art and Technology of Field Work" (1970) to show the uses of cameras and tape recorders in research. Emile de Brigard (1975) wrote "The History of Ethnographic Film," to trace the historical process of the films that have been made to present people in society. Today, there is a group of "ethnographic" filmmakers working in different departments of anthropology or independently all over the world. John Collier Jr., who served on the Farm Security Administration (FSA) led by Roy E. Stryker to collect pictures depicting the people of the United States in their context during a national economic depression, was one of the pioneers in visual anthropology. In eight years (1935–1943) the FSA collected over 270,000 visual documents significant to the emotion and detail of the rural people. John Collier Jr. later worked with Ecuadorean anthropologist Aníbal Buitrón (1949) to visually (film) document culture change: *The Awakening Valley* (see Collier and Collier 1986).

Over the years of this century, anthropologist/filmmakers have produced a number of *etic* cultural films and *emic* films "for," "by," and "of" the people. The Rundstrom, Rundstrom, and Bergum (1971) motion picture *The Path* was one motion picture to use the intentional *emic* aesthetic group-input for the creation of an exact story board, film process, and outcome review. Marilyn Ravičz says of the Rundstrom experiment:

> For example, Rundstrom *et al.* 1973 use both film and ethnography in order to analyze a dramatic ritual situation which has a heavy aesthetic investiture in symbolic movements, objects, and kinaesthetic aspects (1974:433).

Many ethnographic motion pictures have dealt with biographies, but usually the approach and methods are obscure (perhaps the methods are not even mentioned unless there is a written anthropological review published). Commercial films have been successful with biographies offering a rich technical finish such as the motion picture *Gandhi*.

63

Since professional cinema and television are institutions, the anthropologist is intimidated by film making. Perhaps anthropologists believe their films cannot match the polished format and technique of the *cineastes*. Still, people would like to see ethnographic films (de Heusch 1962).

Robert B. Edgerton and L. L. Langness ask in *Methods and Styles in the Study of Culture* (1977:86):

> It is a curious fact of contemporary anthropology, however, that ethnographic films, which so obviously involve selection, editing, often deliberate acting and other distortions of reality, are so eagerly and widely accepted by the public, when novels and even personal accounts of fieldwork are not.

A few in the discipline of anthropology continue to argue that film is a useful technique that should be put into practice in usual research. A simple camera allows the anthropologist to handle limited but adequate visual recordings. In an article entitled *The Short Take*, Ivo Strecker (1982) recommends that ethnographers handle easy-to-use technology.

> Ethnographers seem to think that their films would look too
> primitive compared to the products made with sophisticated equipment.
> Yet, I think anyone who would like to make a film should overcome this
> fear and take the simple camera into his or her hands.
>
> ...What gives a film (and similar devices such as charts, maps, graphs,
> pictorial diagrams, etc.) its value is, among other things, the economy
> by which it shows 'how things are'. This economy can never be introduced at the late stage of editing, but has to be at work already at the
> early stage of shooting (*ibid.*:10).

Strecker goes on to say the ethnographer using film becomes more conscious of the "reductionist character" of a model. He says "A take is 'intense' when it shows what it tries to show in an optimal way" (*ibid.*:11). He also wrote, that in order to touch on the "presence of mind," the filmmaker must photograph a certain length of scene just to the right point where meaning develops in a total event. The tool or the type of camera and technique selected should match the intention of the research to keep the researcher close to the point of intended expression.

In a conversation with Margaret Mead about camera work, Gregory Bateson commented "of the things that happen, the camera is only going to record one percent anyway" (Brand 1977:78). Gregory Bateson presented three kinds of cine camera utilizations in anthropology, which comply with what Strecker has expressed as the mindful use of the camera. First, there is the photographic record intended as an art form. That is to say, the film records for information and art specifically "relevant at the time." Then, there is the genre of the ethnographic art film, which includes native meanings and film methods, without an explicit presentation of how the motion picture was produced. And third, there is the method of utilizing a camera in a fixed position "...and not paying attention to it" (*ibid.*:79–80). The last technique is most popular among clinical psychiatrists who use video cameras to record continuous sessions with patients (see Scheflen 1973). Each procedure has specific uses depending on how ethnographers intentionally explore the possibility of film in cluture (Balikei 1992).[1]

The making of Sinhalese life account films has been a community project. The filmic scenes became bundles of research and visual relationships. The narrative on film became a linear representation of a multidimensional life. In the course of filming, the actual life reflection was flattened into a presentational visual form. But in each case, the eventual finished motion picture stands as repository to the participant and/or as a cultural statement for the archives of the community.

The Filmic Portrait: A Monastic Case Study

As the individual is the unit of observation in this work, the motion picture of the person is a composition of psychological realities in an aesthetic arrangement. This includes personal thoughts to cultural ways of doing things. In the process of making a visual document, or written one, the individual must be maintained in a genuine and personal way. The headmonk arranged his life experiences through his process of traditional Buddhist mental organization. By this style he made certain selections in the writing of his biography—which could be used as a film treatment. He had to keep his audience in mind which he anticipated to be monks, village laity, and foreign audiences.

As a "script writer," the headmonk conceptualized his world in a way that would be acceptable to his audience. He went through the visualiza-

---

[1] For discussions on the use of film see: Mead and MacGregor 1951, Preloran 1975, and Heider 1976, 1991. The current survey of motion picture in the Sinhalese commercial context is in Ranee Chatherine Saverimuttu's (1971) *The Development of the Ceylonese Cinema: A Historical Survey of Films and Personalities from 1947–1967 Taking into Account Past Trends and Future Possibilities.*

For related "ethnographic" motion pictures see Yvonne Hanneman's (1973) *The Work of Gomis* an exorcist in the Southern Province of Śrī Lankā; and *Kataragama — A God for All Seasons* (1973) on Granada Television's Disappearing World Series (see Peter Loizos' appraisal in the *American Anthropologist*, 1980:573–593).

tion process of imagination—what the Sinhalese author Rosemary Rogers (Hendrickson 1979:8) has termed the "mind-movie." The researchers also had to conceptualize on paper what the headmonk was expressing. Together, the headmonk and the researchers had to conceptualize memory images into a film treatment. Whether the headmonk was present or not for the filming, there was no real change in his basic composition. The transfer process from script to the motion picture production engaged the headmonk's ideas, Sinhalese aesthetics, and the researcher's handling of the situation to make an aesthetic representative vision of the headmonk's remembered life. The features of personality, role, and community action were listed and checked for validity by the village community.

In the monastic film-document, the headmonk was filmed in his normative community. The individual personality was generalized to include the relationship of the participant and his role as being a monk. The village community at large accepted the film as a "real" visual image. Yet, the motion picture was acknowledged to be made from a certain perspective. The village community at large shared Jacques Maquet's view (1964:51):

> There is no picture without a perspective, that is to say, not taken
> from a definite point. . .It is the fact that the anthropologist perceives
> the social phenomena he studies not from nowhere but from a certain
> point of view, which is his existential situation.

When a photograph is presented, the observer first, makes self-interpretation; second, finds the main point of the message and; third, translates a symbolic statement. There is a mental explanation of each stage so that it may be analysed into a simple series. The photographic explanation may be carried in any direction the observer wishes. Since a photograph is multi-vocal, it acts as a "symbolic" or an "artistic message" with degrees of ambiguity. Even a "straight forward" press photograph has its many nuances beyond the meaning of the "objective" statement.

By the very nature of the photographic art, the built-in limitations of the camera make the photograph a created image from a specific perspective. This fact is not demeaning to the photograph; it is the photographic technique that should be understood when observing a photograph. Once the art is understood for what it is, then the photograph can be seen for a purpose. Camera work must be seen from a point of view. Meaning changes in the camera tilt, location, zoom lens and so on which will "change" the representation of significant events and personages (Worth and Adair 1975:5). It is the art technique of the camera person and editor which make their pictorial interpretation of objectivity. A photographic process is honest in-so-far as it is displayed with open intention and method.

Photography is basically a *tool* to convey images;[2] and its technical limitations (e.g., perspective) should be expressed to the observers.

The film of the headmonk was not an unbiased objective presentation, it was programmed from various elements in the traditions of monastic life. The headmonk and the temple aesthetics manifested an array of cultural impressions. A cluster of this aesthetic tradition should be listed as such: first, chronology in proper order as in the life of the great sage (i.e., Buddha); second, linear presentation as one thing follows another in the proper life sequence; third, formality in bearing ones character as in the case of the discipline of monks and the arrangement of temple space; fourth, the use of warm and cool colors as expressed in the temple paintings; and fifth, the pageantry and ceremony of main events as witnessed and regarded in a traditional life. An example of monastic research rules are as follows:

For the propagation of his teachings, Buddha directed his disciples to conform to guidance under these rules:

(a) A good preacher should in ordinary discourse make them [rules] gradual i.e., commence with *dānakatham, silakatham,* etc.

(b) Observe sequence (*pariyāyadassāvi*) in the details composing a theme.

(c) Use words of compassion (*anuddayatam paticca katham*).

(d) Avoid irrelevant matters (*nāmisantaram katham*).

(e) Make his speeches free from caustic remarks against other people (see Gard 1961:64).

A collection of paintings filled the temple *budu gē* (image house). One painting gave way to another, sequencing the elements of the Buddha's life or scenes of Sinhalese culture. Sometimes, the traditional scenes were independent panels or the images were fluid in a linear direction without framed divisions. As the Buddha was a great story teller, the monks in the monastery followed the same tradition in reciting the model Sinhalese stories. Against the yellow, red, green, or blue wall backgrounds, the monks echoed in the image house the living past as represented in the paintings (see Karunaratne 1948, Wray *et al.* 1972, Ven. Sarada 1991, Seneviratna 1992). The Sinhalese aesthetic intention operates in a similar fashion as in Thai temple art as expressed by Elizabeth Wray *et al.* (1972:11):

---

[2] Don Farber (1987) in his *Taking Refuge in L.A.: Life in a Vietnamese Buddhist Temple*, produced a visual study of many years experience of sensitivity and intentional participation with a Buddhist community. Paolo Chiozzi (1989) has written in *Visual Anthropology* a solid record, reviewing the discipline with special emphasis on Poland and Italy with a general bibliography.

The beauty of Siamese religious painting is not intended to please the eye as an end in itself but to enlist people's attention in order to tell them a story.

From the vision of the ethnographers there runs a stream of interpretation. The interpretation takes the shape of "the one most satisfactory to the mind...[the field researcher's]... knowledge of anthropology, his intellectual skill, his imagination are important assets in that interpretation" (Maquet 1964:52).

My concept of this ethnography was the making of a cultural document in an aesthetic way. The step-by-step procedures followed the aesthetics of the encounters in the course of making the ethnography. The written accounts and films were intended to encompass a vision. The research included an ethnographic understanding of the lay and monastic communities; in this case a monastic stay for the sufficient understanding of the daily happenings. Then the process of keeping notes and making still photographs took place in order to preclude a "mental film" order through the imagination. The film-writing was staged with personal advice from the monks. The actual ethnographic-film making was simply a physical construction of the mind's picture—a continuous series of mental pictures to tell a story. The story was framed and constructed by a method of personal interaction in the "usual context" of the monastic community.

This research was an experiment into the ways of presenting ethnography using life histories, and in so doing, to illustrate the way the traditional Sinhalese belief system has healing tendencies. The method employed, a self reflexive attempt to use film as a procedure to track the steps to the outcome as a study which produces a motion picture as an "emic" cultural document, is steeped in native interpretations coming from Śrī Lankā. The process of native integration into anthropological research was part of the end (see also Norman 1991). The parameters of field limitations have in a sense constructed the outcome: patching up material in some way would be distorting unless the outcome was to be molded into a special form with entertainment film quality or something for journalistic interests. I work from the emergent approach with a concern for the *utility* of the work for the participants, as well as the general knowledge of culture.

*   *   *

The research encoding process for tracking the cultural dimensions is a complementary system which requires knowledge in aesthetic sensibilities (Ven. Gnānissara 1993) such as *rasa*, and considerings on the meaning of cultural techniques and actions which are conveyed in daily life and ritual (Schechner 1990) which energize and motivate people or which just stand as cultural markers (see Rundstrom 1992). My description is not a total ethnography, but a partial treatment of the subject stemming basically from the life histories presented here. I have chosen life histories because I believe that not only *what* a person knows should be displayed, but also how a person has come to face the issues of knowledge.

Salient Feature Life Accounts

The Relationships

...Einstein's laws took the place of Newton's. For Relativity derives
essentially from the philosophic analysis which insists that there is not
a fact and an observer, but a joining of the two in an observation.

—Jacob Bronowski 1962:83

As I have expressed the act of life history writing is a *relationship* and
task performance between the life history writer and subject, I will present
three life accounts.

(1) Monk: the headmonk of the Atulamuni Vihāraya, Hanchāpola.

(2) Deity-shrine Official: the chief administrator of the Kataragama
    Dēvāle, Badulla.

(3) Exorcist: the exorcist/dance master of Akurugoda.

The title of this presentation, *Masks*, denotes an institutional behavioral role for expected personal display. This expected behavior is a condition which sanctions the person for a life in society. The ethnographer
also has an expected behavioral role as researcher regardless of personal
idiosyncrasies. So, each recorded ethnography or life account has a common connection with the characteristics of the participants in ethnographic
association.

Ethnography
(Life History)

Ethnographer
and Association of Advisors

Monk/ Deity-shrine Official/ Exorcist

For my presentation of the written accounts, I have used a method
employed by Theodore F. Harris who wrote *Pearl S. Buck: A Biography*,
1969. Harris wrote the biography in association and consultation with
Pearl Buck. The process took five years (of which two years were spent
in writing the manuscript). The author recalls "I should like to have had

seventy–six years to write this book; perhaps then I would have been able to record each detail of a life which at this point has taken that long to live" (Harris 1969:13). Harris spent hours tape recording her life account; and the audio-record became the design for the book. After the words of Pearl Buck, Harris includes his own statements as his entries in the story:

> How does a life begin? Pearl S. Buck has compared a book's beginning to the creation of a star in the heavens. A swirl of particles in the skies, a swirl of ideas in the vast space of one's mind, gather to form a substance. The process describes the creation of a life, as well. An idea is born in the mind of a man; a hope, developing into desire, grows into reality; love for a woman takes form in a child. A living creature thus begins its long trek through life (*ibid.*:17).

And then after the author's statements, the recorded words of Pearl Buck appear (designated with a vertical line in the margin of that book) to continue the flow of the text: "Of her birth Pearl Buck says with characteristic insistence:"

> I remember when I was born. I am sure I remember. How else can I account for the intimate knowledge I have always had of my mother's house? I have never lived there for more than a few weeks at a time, and not many times. The first time I walked into it on my own feet, I was already nine years old. Yet already I knew every room that I was to see. I knew how the grapevine grew over the portico. I knew when I entered the door that the parlor was to the left and the library to the right. True, a later generation had changed the library to another use, but for me it was the library and music room. It was still the music room, where a musical family gathered to play organ and violin and to sing (*ibid.*:18).

Most of the biography is autobiography with connecting passages and reflections by the personal authorship of Harris, who said, "I can think of no one with whom I would rather have breakfast, luncheon, cocktails or dinner, or sight-see or drive or go on a picnic or to a coffeehouse or a concert..." (*ibid.*:14).

In a later biography on Pearl Buck, Theodore Harris (1971) utilizes her personal letters. In that text, sub-titled "Her Philosophy as Expressed in Her Letters," the author writes personal and historical statements which connect the letters in a series. *Volume One* of Pearl Buck's biography drew from the recollections vocalized by the woman interviewed over years for the specific purpose of writing a biography and *Volume Two* from "historic" letters which were compiled later.

My method proceeded from the time when I studied monastic life. Then I followed the methodological approach established for the head-monk's life history research (see Blundell 1979, 1991 and for other motion pictures 1980, 1981). My studies were based on the participants' input and discussion as to the rationale, procedure, and outcome of the work (see Ruby 1977). I have not dealt with long-term accumulation of footage as in the case of John Marshall *et al.* (1980) from the time of Laurence K. Marshall in 1951 through 1990 among the !Kung, or "San," in the Kalahari Desert region of Namibia and Botswana.[1] I did select photo-album materials (see Chalfen 1983) when available, as seen of the *basnāyaka nilamē* on page 99 in this sectioin on life accounts, and for the utility of the research visual requirements. Visual element and flow were based on emic aesthetic choices (Rundstrom *et al.* 1973).

In each case study, I have collected autobiographical accounts in just a few pages of words spoken or written by each participant. In my presentation here, I give an overview of the ethnographic situation—and, then the life account. The life account is italicized. Then I include my own short statements from my experience with the research, tradition, and participant. My statements are not to be an analysis of the participant's words—but the statements should be read as a for-the-reader commentary to the life accounts.[2]

In terms of the life histories, I have used a basic frame of reference based on the traditional Buddhist values of balance and harmony in terms of daily life (de Certeau 1984). Buddhism in every dimension is a mental discipline. The Pāli canon confirms this in the concept of *samajīvikatā* (balanced livelihood) for the Buddhist laity (see the text Paṭhamasamajīvī Sutta). A balanced life means life should not be excessive in any direction of livelihood.

---

[1] Refer to page 48, note 3.

[2] See Langness' selection from *Two Leggings: The Making of a Crow Warrior* by Peter Nabokov to illustrate life history procedure in his *Other Fields, Other Grasshoppers* (1977:61-72).

Buddha and Monastery

...for Sinhalese the Buddha is cognitively human but affectively divine.
—Richard Gombrich 1971:9

In Sinhalese society, the traditional belief system, Buddhism, is called *buddhāgama*. This belief system of the Buddha is a religion based on the teaching of the great sage—Gotama Buddha (or Siddhārtha Gautama). The historic person was born as prince Siddhārtha at Lumbini, Nepal in the 6th Century B.C. He was one of a series of enlightened men going through the cycle of rebirths (*samsāra*). Today, among the Sinhalese, the stories of the 550 past lives of this particular Buddha are in the written collection called the *Jātaka*. The visual representation of the stories are found in Buddhist temples at the image house (*budu gē*).

> The Buddhist temple is essentially a place of worship... It is however doubtful whether this sacred atmosphere is always maintained within the premises of a temple...The assimilation of certain rituals into pure forms of religious observation has given rise to a large number of festivals, ceremonies and processions based in the temple. In recent times there has been a tendency to modernize them by the addition of various diversions combining worship with entertainment. What takes place at an average temple on some of the more important religious occasions is this type of diversion which can easily attract a crowd to the temple. In a sense, this situation helps a generation belonging to a traditional society dominated by religious practices to find a balance between conventional religious obligations and modern tendencies to seek entertainment as an essential part of day to day life (Bandara 1972:46).

The stories of the Buddha are paramount in Buddhist society as the Buddha stands for the ideal person. The life of the Buddha was the model for the rendition of a Buddhist monk in the headmonk's motion picture (1979 and 1980). At the Atulamuni Vihāraya, Hanchāpola, the image house interior was complemented with different episode paintings of the Buddha.

The Buddha preached a *path* (a way of life) which led the person to attain *prajñā* (higher wisdom without content) by purging the mind of empirical knowledge, ego, and all desire. *Sammuti* (conventional) and *paramattha* (absolute) were two forms of truth *(sacca)* recognized all along, and centuries after the passing of the great sage, although writers interpreted his discourses according to the linguistic usages accepted by the intelligentsia of their times. The Pāli expression *sammuti sacca* literally means the con-

77

ventional truth. These truths formed the universal truth and conventional usage of truth through discourse to demonstrate the message of the Buddha for followers.

Life for the monks after the passing away of the Buddha became established and residential in time. Devoted monks of learning and social commitment worked from a common site near a lay village or in a town. These monks maintained their boundaries (*sīmā*) within a social context to continue education and ritual for themselves and the laity. The laity supported the monastery as a nexus for culture. The tradition was preserved in the temple compound for the welfare of the society at large. Donors (*dāyakas*) or (*dāyakā*) set the pattern of giving to maintain the monastic philosophy of patience, non-violence, learning, high moral standards, and stability. The people who gave to the monastery obtained spiritual merit (*pin*) which could be treated as an act which placed the donor on a spiritually higher plane, valuable for a better rebirth. The monastic donation (*dāna*) symbolized the gift given without anything in return. The monks, according to the way of the Buddha, always received such offerings from the laity. In turn the monasteries became institutional repositories of wealth, safe with the renouncing monks.

Buddhism has played an overarching role in Sinhalese history. The *saṅgha* (order of monks) has been sanctioned by the state from king to village chief since the arrival of Buddhism. Monks took on the role as tradition guards and admonishers for laymen. They were community dwellers concerned with the welfare of the society. Monks also remained isolated in the monastery or retreated to the forest for solitude and meditation. So, there was the *world guiding quality* and the *world fleeing quality* among *saṅgha* members.

> The Dhamma has two wheels: One (*dhammacakka*) that envisions a lonely, individual quest and another (*ānācakka*) that is hardly 'self-referring' and speaks of political and domestic order [of supremacy and protective power] (Kemper 1980:195).

The monastic compound (*vihāraya*) comprises three basic structures matching the *triple gem*: Buddha-*dhamma-saṅgha*. In Bandaranayake's study (1974) of Anurādhapura monastic sites (200 B.C.–1000 A.D.), there is an elaborate presentation of building types and their functions. The presentation begins with,

> ... the essential requirements of a [Sinhalese Buddhist] monastery...: i. a *cetiya* [as a repository for relics (*dhātu*)], ii. the provision of suitable facilities for the exposition of the Dhamma, and iii. accommodation for the *Saṅgha*... We have, therefore, categorized the threefold architec-

tural division which derives from this as i. Shrines and Sanctuaries, ii. Ecclesiastical Buildings, and iii. Residential Buildings (*ibid.*:27).

In Sinhalese Buddhist monasteries, the wealth has become a tenure system of lands and resources. People depend on the honesty of the monks (especially the headmonk) for the safeguard of their offerings. Today, as in the past, the offerings are essential: the food, materials, and laity sons. Everyone expects the monks to maintain their rules of discipline (*Vinaya*) in order to preserve ritual sanctions, and qualitative socio-economic conditions. The responsibility and tasks are demanding for the monks who search for a life of peace and tranquility away from the bustle of society.

An individual monk can not lead an anonymous existence. Even forest dwelling monks in Śrī Lankā learn from Buddhist society and act upon sequences of acceptable behavior sanctioned by that structure to be a forest dwelling monk. People from surrounding villages donate food and supplies for recluse monks, who later become well known recluses in the society (see Yalman 1962).

Monk

Monks [*def.*] A *bhikkhu* is one who has received the Higher Ordination (*upasampadā*) in a Buddhist monastic order (*saṅgha*) that is based on the acceptance of the Code of Discipline (*Vinaya*). In this context, however, the Commentary says: '*Bhikkhu* is given here as an example for those dedicated to the practice of the Teaching....Whosoever undertakes that practice...is here comprised under the term *bhikkhu.*

— Nyanaponika Thera 1975:132

The literary ideal of a monk acting in the traditional Buddhist setting could be drawn from the *Psalms of Early Buddhists: The Sisters, the Brethren* (i.e., *Thera-Therī-Gāthā*) translated from the original Pāli (1964) by Mrs. Rhys Davids or *Buddhist Monastic Life According to the Texts of the Theravāda Tradition* by Mohan Wijayaratna (1990). My image of monks comes from my living and interaction with them. I have not entirely relied on the textual ideal of the way a monk should behave. Also, my orientation comes from historic and contemporary case studies (see Dutt 1962, Yalman 1962, Ames 1966, Nash 1966, Spiro 1970, Tambiah 1970, Gombrich 1971, Evers 1972, Obeyesekere 1972, Maquet 1975a.b, Seneviratne 1978, Gothóni 1982, Carrithers 1983, Bechert and Gombrich 1984, Tambiah 1984, and Holt 1991). I will present a monk as he speaks about his own life.

From the earliest Buddhist tradition it has been mentioned that there are four kinds of monks. The first is the *path-finder* (*magga jino*) who

searches only for salvation (*nibbāna*) to win the *path*. Second, there is
the *path-pointer* (*magga uddesaka*) who teaches the ethics of the tradition
dhamma and universal phenomenon. Third, there is the kind of monk who
just *lives-on-the-path* (*magge jīvi*) without working. Fourth, there is the
path-spoiler (*magga dushi*) who wastes the value of discipline by breaking
the laws of the *sangha*. The *sangha* has always accepted different kinds of
monk characteristics. The monk I have selected, or the one who chose me,
is a *path-pointer* as usually is the case for a village headmonk in Śrī Lankā.

To describe the headmonk of Hanchāpola village temple, Punchi Banda
Meegaskumbura selected this Pāli verse:

Eni jangham kisam dhiram appaharam alolupam
Siham eekacaram nāgam kāmesu anapekkhitam
Upasamkamma pucchāmi katham dukkhā pamuccare
Panca kāmagunā loke mano chatthā pavedino
Ettha chandam virājetva evam dukkhā pamuccare

— *Samyutta Nikāya*

Translation:
Limbed like the antelope, lean, vigorous,
In diet sober, craving not t'indulge
Like lion, lonely faring elephant,
Indifferent to the calls of senses: — Lo! we,
Into thy presence come that we may ask
How we from every ill may be set free?

— *Kindred Sayings*

Ven. H. Gnānavansa Thero 1979

81

Loku Hāmuduruvō

Name: Ven. Hanchāpola Gnānavansa Thero

Native Village: Hanchāpola

Residing Village: Hanchāpola

Date of Birth: April 24th, 1902

Caste: Govigama[1] (cultivators)

Time and place of record: This account was written in Sinhala by the
headmonk in mid-November 1978 at the
Hanchāpola Temple (Atulamuni Vihāraya).

Account written by Ven. Hanchāpola Gnānavansa Thero:

*I was born in Hanchāpola, Village Headman's Division No. 33, of Yati-
gaha Pattu, Hālpitigam Kōralé, Colombo District, Śrī Lankā. I was born
on the twenty-fourth of April 1902.*

The headmonk is very precise here in his statement of birth.

*My mother was Upāsika Dunnegedara Sophia Nona. My father was H.
A. Daniel Appūhamy, a native physician. We had ten brothers and sisters
in our family; of them seven were sisters and three were brothers. My third
brother was the late Ven. Hanchāpola Śrī Vimalavaṇsa Thero, the Deputy
Chief [of the Rāmañña Nikāya] and the incumbent of Dharmākīrtyārama
[temple] of Kollupitiya [in Colombo]. I am the eighth of the family children.
Of my brothers and sisters, only five are still living.*

Here the monk's mother is mentioned as a lay-devotee (*upāsika*) of
a temple. Both mother and father have Christian and Sinhalese names.
It was felt that under British rule, a Christian name was very honorable.
For example, the mother's name Dunnegedara Sophia Nona is a cultural
collection: Dunnegedara is the Sinhalese house name, Sophia is a European
name, and Nona is Portuguese for lady.

*As a youngster, I received my primary education at the Vitānamulla
Buddhist Mixed School. After the fourth grade, I joined the Nugawala English School [near Veyangoda] in 1912. After that I joined St. Lawrence
College at Wellawatta [Colombo] for higher secondary education. After
spending one year studying there, very successfully, such subjects as math-*

---

[1] *Govigama* (cultivators of the land) is the highest caste among the Sinhalese
and it is the most numerous group in Śrī Lankā.

ematics, English, Sinhala, and so on, I left St. Lawrence College to join Ānanda College, Colombo. There, was where I received the last years of my education as a layman.

In childhood, several schools were attended, both Christian and Buddhist—private and public. His school, Ānanda College, was famous for high school Buddhist studies and the principal was an American. The boy's elder brother, who was already a respected monk in the Rāmañña Nikāya, influenced him in a subtle way as a role-model to follow for an established way of life.

It was my elder brother, Ven. Hanchāpola Vimalavaṇsa Thero, the chief incumbent of Dharmākīrtyārama of Kollupitiya, who supported and encouraged me to study while I was in Colombo.

An elder brother who was headmonk at Kollupitiya, Colombo, guided the youth towards the Buddhist discipline. But still, the boy was restless in the *urban* environment.

Colombo has its own socio-architectural context known as *kolamba* in Sinhala, with its own character based on trade. It is a place where a suburban network of people aspire to have a way of life which is mixed between the cultures of the *best* between East and West. But, every Sinhalese Colombo family has ties to the countryside. Colombo people will always journey to the rural areas to visit friends, to obtain cultural items, to attend ritual occasions, or to gather fresh food. The agrarian system is always close at hand. "Commercial" things are found in Colombo and "country" items come from rural areas.

By this time, I was about sixteen years old. There was an enthusiastic resurgence of Buddhism in and around Colombo District and Hālpitigam Kōrale. The pioneer of this interest was Ven. Mudagamuve Śrī Nivāsa Thero. His dhamma expositions and admonitions were instrumental in directing my life towards a new path. My mind was bent on becoming a Buddhist monk. Then, I decided to join the saṅgha [Buddhist order] within the Rāmañña Nikāya of Śrī Lankā. On the ninth day of April 1919, at 7:10 in the morning, I entered novicehood at the Atulamuni Vihāraya of Hanchāpola. My preceptor was Ven. Mudagamuve Śrī Nivāsabha Mahāthera, and the teachers were Ven. Hissälle Ñānodaya Mahāthera, head of the Rāmañña Nikāya and the chief incumbent of Saraswati Piriveṇa of Balagalla, and Ven. Yatagama Śrī Ñānakkhandha Mahāthera, provincial chief and head of the Śrī Dharmarāja Piriveṇa of Nedalagamuva.

This statement explores the fascination of Buddhist learning and religious debates in the populated southwestern area of Śrī Lankā. The monk shows great respect as he names his teachers of the discipline. But, he fails to mention the experience about when he ran away from Colombo to work with some manual laborers to the north (Nikaveratiya). The boy contracted malaria in that jungle area. After a while, his relatives found him and brought him back to his native village.

The monk related to me that, in his teenage youth, he tried different kinds of occupation at the training stage, but he was dissatisfied with the various lay disciplines (e.g., the practice of rice cultivation, Sinhalese medicine). So then, on occasion, he went to the temple with his grandfather. After a while the boy became increasingly aware of formal Buddhism.

I think the resolution to become a member of the *saṅgha* was made because the boy saw the refinement of the monastic discipline. As a boy he observed the great respect monks were given by laymen. Even a novice monk is given great respect by his relations and elders in the village. The boy aspired to achieve a cultural and spiritual position.

The monk remembers the exact time to the minute of his lower ordination. This is because ceremonies in Srī Laṅkā are timed to the correct auspicious moment selected from an astrological chart by an expert concerning the planets. That moment is mentioned as one of the favorable times of life (e.g., the moment of birth, and so on).

The boy joined the Rāmañña Nikāya, one of the three Sinhalese Buddhist denominations: Siyam Nikāya (i.e., from Thailand), Rāmañña and Amarapura *nikāyas* (named after provincial areas of Burma). The Siyam Nikāya was established in the mid-18th Century under the reign of Kīrti Srī Rājasiṅgha. Monks of the Theravāda tradition coming from Mahāvihāra, Anurādhapura, flourished prior to the Siamese tradition. It was when the Buddhist order declined in Srī Laṅkā that the tradition of ordination was reintroduced, which had originally come from Srī Laṅkā. By royal decision, monks were requested to come from Ayodya in Thailand, insuring a sufficient number of them to continue the practice of official ordination. Ven. Srī Saranankara Sangharāja advised the king to secure the high ordained monks from Thailand. Once the Siyam Nikāya was operational, royal authority allowed only high caste (*govigama*) members to enter. The *nikāya* was centered in Kandy in two chapters: Asgiriya and Malwatta (see Ven. Wachissara 1961). In the late 18th Century, Ven. Ñanavimalatissa Thero went to Amarapura in Burma to be confirmed a second time as monk under the Burmese rules of high ordination. In 1803, he founded the Amarapura Nikāya, which was less centered than the Siyam Nikāya. The *nikāya* accepted members from every caste. About thirty sub-sects of this *nikāya* developed nation wide.

The Rāmañña Nikāya was founded in 1835 as a conservative movement which interpreted the rules of monks (*Vinaya*), coming from the original Buddhist disciples of ancient times. There was a famous debate between Ven. Atthadassi Thero and his followers and representatives from both Siyam Nikāya and Amarapura Nikāya. The main question was: When does the ceremony for the rainy season sojourn (*vassāna* or *vas*) commence? Ven. Atthadassi Thero illustrated his point with his background of astronomy to establish the exact date of the religious rite.

The Rāmañña Nikāya monks live only with the essential possessions for simple living and they denounce the deity system. These monks can be recognized from the other *nikāyas* simply because they carry a leaf umbrella when in public.

> Monastic reform is a recurrent phenomenon: periodic renovation has been a means of maintaining a continuity of Buddhist traditions down through the centuries. The idea of reform is therefore not new to Sinhalese Buddhism. The ideas of today's reformers are new, however, and so is the external setting (Ames 1969:75).

In Hanchāpola, as an exclusive high caste (*govigama*) village, the Siyam Nikāya prevailed until the turn of the century. But, it seems that some negligence of the temple on the part of the monks caused the village laity to invite Rāmañña Nikāya monks who were using the temple as a retreat to stay permanently. On a permanent basis, the temple was developed by the leadership of the Rāmañña Nikāya monks who ordained the boy.

Since then, I was known by the ordained name of Hanchāpola Gnānavansa. From that time, I started my basic religious training under the guidance of my preceptors and teachers. I lived at Saraswati Pirivena,[2] Balagalla, and Śrī Sākyasinhārama Vihāraya, Mābotalé.

The novice monk had to learn the strict religion and Pāli at the *pirivenas* in his immediate district. The two schools mentioned in the text are near Hanchāpola. While at the *pirivena*, the monk heard a verse which he remembered from childhood. Although he did not know the meaning of the verse, it was recognized much later and learned.

Puṇḍarikaṃ yāthā vaggu toyena nūpalimpati
Nūpalimpati kāmena sammā sambuddha sāvako

---

[2] A *pirivena* is a religious school in or near a monastery primarily established for the education of the novice monk (*sāmanēra*) to the way of the Buddha in terms of classical texts, language training (e.g., Pāli and Sanskrit), including English and the humanities.

Translation:
As a beautiful lotus does not adhere to the water, so
also a disciple of the perfectly Enlightened-One would
not be overwhelmed by the pleasures of the senses.

The event of the *verse* marks a transition or a *turning* in the child's
life as he comes to monastic realization.

This verse was not mentioned directly in the written life account; but it
was revealed in interviews and thus presented in the monk's motion picture.

*It was the twenty-ninth of December 1922 when I received my high or-
dination involving the higher precepts. This ceremony was performed at the
sīmāva [sacred space] at the Pollatu-modara ferry of Mātara by the mandate
of the Mahā Nākaya Thera of the Rāmañña Nikāya and other monks. My
preceptor for high ordination was Ven. Mahopadhyāya Ōbadakande Śrī Vi-
malānanda Mahāthera. After that, in 1924, I was admitted to Śrī Saddhar-
modaya Piriveṇa at Walapola in Panadure; and I received special training in
religious matters for four years under Ven. Kōdāgoda Upasena Mahāthera,
chief of the Rāmañña Nikāya.*

High ordination (*upasampadā*) is the most supreme ritual for a man
entering the *saṅgha*. This ceremony requires the attendance of five senior
presiding monks. By the 16th Century, the number of ordained monks
had decreased to the level where it was difficult to arrange the ceremony
properly. The re-occurrence of regular *upasampadās* began in the year of
1753 after the Sinhalese king encouraged high ordained monks to come from
Siam (see Hazra 1982).

The ceremony of high ordination took place at a *sīmāva* (sacred space)
for monks in the middle of a river in order to keep the sanctuary from
touching the impure world.

Four years passed as the new monk attended various *piriveṇas*; his
teacher was the chief incumbent (*mahāthera*) of the *nikāya*.

*In 1928, I came back to the Sarasvati Piriveṇa of Balagalla and resided
at the Atulamuni Vihāraya of my native village. While studying at the
piriveṇa, I was also engaged in religious activities in the village. In 1938, I
was invited to be in charge of the affairs of the Śrī Sumana Piriveṇa, Ratnapura. There, I was engaged in conducting religious and national duties.
In 1938, when the Second World War started, I came back to Atulamuni
Vihāraya in order to take charge of the temple.*

The monk faithfully returned to his native village to live and attend
to the neighboring *piriveṇa* just a mile or so away. Then he was called
away again ten years later to manage the affairs of the important Ratna-

pura *piriveṇa*. During the emergency of war (1938–1945), the country was mobilized to support the British effort towards the Pacific and Europe.

At that time, the Sinhalese people were also anticipating their independence during the political ferment in South Asia. Symbols of religion and tradition were actively used as tools for national self-determination.

After joining the saṅgha, I have served as the headmonk of several temples in Śrī Laṅkā. I also have spent my vassāna [rainy sojourn] at different places. Śrī Śākyasinhārama of Mābotalé, Śrī Śumana Vidyalaya of Patakada, Abhināvārama of Muvagama, Ratnapura, Sarasvati Piriveṇa of Balagalla, Atulamuni Vihāraya of Hanchāpola are some of the places where I spent my vassāna on many occasions. Also, I have spent vassāna at the following places: Nedalagamuva, Mavilmada, Nuwara Eliya, Bandarawela, Kollupitiya, Āgarapatana, Bibile, Dēvālegame, Bolagala, Henpitagedara, Ganemulla, and Gampola by the request of the devotees in each place. I wish to record my thanks to all those who encouraged and helped me to carry on my religious duties in those places.

The list of temples indicates the monk served at various temples. The *vassāna* or *vas* occasion is when a monk must leave his monastery to live for sometime (usually three months by tradition) in another spiritual location. Originally, this practice allowed the wandering monks to find shelter and stay of time while the monsoon passed in South Asia. Also, the occasion allowed new blood to attend to the temple establishment.

On four occasions in my life I was able to journey on pilgrimage to India to witness all those holy places where the great sage [Buddha], greatest of the Śākyas, was born, attained enlightenment, expounded his dhamma, and demised. In Laṅkā, I have visited all the holy places except Divāguhāva (where the Buddha reposed during the day time while visiting this country; the actual place has not yet been traced). I have visited Burma once on a pilgrimage to the holy places.

Occasions of pilgrimage allowed the monk to visit the shrines of Śrī Laṅkā and of other Buddhist centers abroad. The monk was impressed by his visit to Burma during the international celebration on the occasion to mark 2500 years after the passing of the Buddha. As an invited guest, he experienced the vastness of Buddhism while participating in the Burmese event. He also mentioned in the Burmese style of receiving food offerings (*dāna*).

In terms of giving alms or *dāna*, which is the offering of fruits, flowers, and cloth or various staples to the shrines or monks, it is an act highly associated with the Buddha and the guardian deities. The belief system is based on giving. It is fundamental in the belief system that people gain and store merit points (*pin*) for their best deeds. The *saṅgha* is based on the support of villagers. In the monastic motion picture, the headmonk and other monks required the temple offering be displayed in the first scene. This is represented by the offering of flowers to the Buddha image. In the motion pictures, the act of giving was suggested to be an initial event in the visual sequences.

India was his *grand tour* of Buddhist shrines where he endured long overland journeys. The monk recalled and demonstrated the way that Tibetan monks repeatedly worship with the body on a board flat in front of the Buddha-gaya Temple (the site where the Buddha gained enlightenment at the *bō*-tree).

My usual place of residence is at Atulamuni Vihāraya of Hanchāpola. At this time, I lead a composed life (viveka) while giving the necessary guidance and admonishment to improve the condition of Atulamuni Vihāraya and neighboring temples to help the devotees improve their moral stature. After taking charge [of this temple], we have completed the dāgāba (cetiya), which holds the Buddha relics, the enclosure of the bō-tree, and the image house, including the image at Atulamuni Vihāraya. We have also constructed the preaching hall, meditation dwelling, sīmāva (uposathāgāra), and dining hall.

The aesthetic philosophy of the monk is developed as he explains that the composed life (*viveka*) is the key to mindful maintenance of life and monastery. The monk arranged his temple space according to terraces corresponding to levels of spiritualness. On the highest level is the pure *dāgāba* (shrine-mound) for the relics or essence of the Buddha. Then, on the second level below, are the meditation abode and image house. On the existing third level below stands the preaching hall (*dhamma sālā*) and *bō*-tree. At a fourth level is the residence house, dining hall, and kitchen of the monks. The *sīmāva* (special chapter house) is on a separate level between the image house and the bathing water-tank. Actually, the monk expressed that if he had the chance to design the temple space from the beginning, he would have placed the image house on the third level, and he would have planted the *bō*-tree on the second level (see following page).

The aesthetic composition of the entire monastery and the ideal format expressed by the monk gave me the impression: just by observing the spatial layout of the temple, it could communicate much about the attitude of monks. Certainly the concept of a tranquil and composed life without anxiety and mental disturbance was working in the physical architectural and garden design. The monastic space seemed to be nicely situated in a park of massive trees and swept grounds.

This is a graphic display of monastic spatial relationships in terms of the Atulamuni Monastery's existing situation and the ideal thought:[3]

existing situation	**ideal format**
relic shrine (*dāgāba*)	relic shrine (*dāgāba*)
image house/meditation abode	*bō*-tree/meditation abode
bō-tree/preaching hall	image house/preaching hall
residence house	residence house

Now, I am seventy-seven years old. My only hope is to lead a composed life while performing all my religious and national obligations; including help to all devotees of mine in order to enhance their moral stature.

The monk told me many times he was interested in two aspects of life: religious performance and national duty. As in the village monk (*grāmavāsi*) tradition, he was people-minded; and, therefore, he worked for the safety, maintenance, and education of the society.

Atulamuni Vihāraya of Hanchāpola is a residential monastery for student monks and teacher monks of Sarasvati Piriveṇa, Balagalla. Those monks who reside here perform their religious tasks enthusiastically for the sake of the devotees of this temple. On special occasions we invite monks from the piriveṇa. All monks of the piriveṇa consider me one of their teachers. As this is the situation, I never had the longing to have my own students as the usual case. However, I have recently ordained two students by the persistent request of my lay devotees. The elder [student] of the two is in charge of the dhamma school of this temple; also he acts as the head of another temple [at Bemmulla]. The second one continues to study as a novice in the piriveṇa. It is not my strategy to give advice all the time to everyone. Model behavior on the part of the elders is the only system of administration that prevails here.

Education is stressed as the most important feature for the up-bringing of youths into society. Here the monk expresses that novice monks consider him as a teacher; yet he does not teach in any particular way. It was his philosophy to *act* with the proper attitude and in the correct behavior of the

---

[3] Ven. Havanpola Ratanasara Thero gave me the following list as an orientation to temple structure which matches an ideal structural form of essential elements:

(1) *saririka*—relics (*dhātu*), *dāgāba*;

(2) *paribhogika*—utilization objects, including *bō*-tree, bowls and robes;

(3) *uddesika*—Buddha statue or symbol.

tradition for others to observe. Just by observing his actions, the students or laymen around him would learn the composed life.

When I look back over my past sixty years as a monk, from this elevated position of seventy-seven years of age, I feel much enraptured. When I see I have been instrumental in instilling something good in a few persons through the morals I have safeguarded and from what I have learned, I feel I have achieved a beneficial life. I have no craving for the outside world. There is nothing for me to oversee. My mind is not burdened. I believe my mental flexibility has allowed me to engage in itinerant journeys around the country to serve people of diverse stations of life.

Even though the monk was very disciplined, he was flexible and subtle in his decision-making process. He also accepted and assisted people of every caste and social position.

The monk was satisfied with his life and about the fact that he assisted individuals, including himself, to a more beneficial life. First, the practice of demonstrating his ability without commanding, and second, the *act* of giving without expecting anything in return (because his giving was a release of burdens) made the monk a suitable administrator and guardian of the belief system.

I insist I should serve the religion and nation as long as I live in order to bring about benefit for the laity in terms of improving their moral fortitude.

The monk lived his life assisting people to find a suitable path within the tradition.

*   *   *

The monk was a disciplined man who arranged his life according to traditional behavior. His actions were very precise as he followed the *Vinaya*. His solo passage in the ocean of change (*saṃsāra*) was not unique in terms of individual monks in the *saṅgha*.

As a brief comparison, the *basnāyaka nilamē*, a deity-shrine administrator, also had religious responsibility, but first, he was married, second, he had a wide range of non-religious experiences, and third, he was not disciplined to a monastic routine.

The exorcist was the most independent in terms of traditional service as he had little administrative work other than his own performances; yet he was burdened, like the *basnāyaka nilamē*, to earn a living for his family and to maintain his physical strength for performance tasks.

The monk was always at ease with his work performance. He rested when he was so inclined and he worked for the community in the most composed manner. As a headmonk, his quality of composed life resounded in a village version of *Thera-Therī-Gāthā* as in the *Poems of Cloister and Jungle*, where a recluse monk expressed the life composed in the solitude of nature.

> When that he makes becomes the path of peace,
> From sorrow free, untarnished and uncorrelated,
> Cleansing from all that doth defile, and severing
> From every bond and gyve, no higher bliss
> Is given to men than this.
>
> —(Davids 1941:85)

The monk, Ven. H. Gnānavansa Thero stayed in his societal monastery or another social accessible temple where he could commune with other monks and laity. The forest life was a dream existence or an ideal practiced by very few individual monks in the Southern Asia area.

The Kataragama Dēvāle
and Basnāyaka Nilamē

The deities of the Sinhalese pantheon form a network under the Buddha. Kataragama is one of the great deities. Kataragama was created in the event of a military campaign between the *dēva* and *asurā*. The *dēva* were suffering under the blows of their enemy, so they appealed to Śiva for assistance. Śiva's answer was in the form of his son Karthikeya or Kataragama, who swiftly defeated the fierce supernatural beings (*asurā*). The young deity became a hero in South Asia (South India and Śrī Lankā). His story in Śrī Lankā is as follows: The deity, son of powerful Śiva and celestial Pārvati, came to Lankā and fell in love with Valli, the daughter of a Veddä (aborigine) chief. The couple lived together in the forest among the hills just east of the Menik Ganga (Stream of Gems). The site was peaceful. Kataragama made it his home for his sojourns in Lankā. He stayed with Valli Amma; even though, his first wife Devayānaya resided in India.

In terms of iconography, Kataragama is portrayed either as a boy or as an adult. As a child, the deity stands alone with a weapon. As an adult, he is handsome and rides a peacock and bears auspicious weapons. Sometimes he is seen with one face or he could have six faces. The six faces seem to be a later development as they are not manifest in ancient temples (see Jouveau-Dubreuil 1937:44–47). The wives sometimes ride with the deity. Devayānaya would be seated on the left of the deity. Her skin is fair and her personal vehicle is the elephant (as in the case of the deity Indra). Valli Amma would be seated on the right side of Kataragama. Her skin is dark and her personal vehicle is the lion (similar to the mount of Indra's wife, Indrāni).

At the same site of the hero Kataragama, the Sinhalese king Duṭugāmuṇu, according to the chronicle *Kanda Māla* journeyed to the divine site where he underwent penances for divine assistance in order to be confident of victory against the reigning Tamil King Elāra in the north. Since that time, the site has been a national and religious shrine imbued with the power of deity and the privilege of an ancient Sinhalese king who won the country for the Sinhalese people:

> ...the King [Duṭugāmuṇu] erected...an entrance gateway of seven steps
> [to high buildings], as thanks offering to the God of war [Kataragama].
> On the site, he erected a shrine to Ganesh, a kitchen for making offer-
> ings, an alter for flowers, and a kovil [Hindu temple] for Goddess Pattini

93

[female Guardian deity of the fields and provinces]. Four furlongs off, he built the Kiri Vihāra [*dāgāba*] and formed parks (*Udyāna*) round the seven sacred hills (from the chronicle *Kanda Māla*; Raghavan 1962:62).

During July and August, individuals and groups journey for the Äsaḷa season to Kataragama, where thousands assemble from different regions of South Asia for the activities of the deity shrine. The Śrī Lankā *dēvāles* "celebrate" the deities. Processions (*perahäras*) are conducted in festival spirit demonstrated in an array of elephants and lights. The purpose is to offer a *pūjā*, which is currently an act of respect in the form of an offering of coconuts, plantains, or flowers; or a behavior of penance by rolling in the hot dust around the shrine, holding a coconut in the hands outstretched, dancing *kāvāḍi* in a state of trance, firewalking, or hanging by hooks from a wooden frame with wheels. The term *pūjā* comes from Sanskrit which means the *peaceful* offering of fruits and flowers to the deity of the shrine or temple. Pilgrims reach the shrine area at the banks of the Menik Ganga, where they bathe and dress in "new" white or saffron/red clothes before entering the sacred space.

Entry through the grand arched gateway (*makara toraṇa*) into the grounds shows the pilgrim a sight of people in ecstatic states of devotional interaction (*bhakti*) with a personalized deity.[1] Castes are representative from the South Indian Hindu and Sinhalese Buddhist systems. Pilgrims stir the air with camphor smoke and offer prayers to the shrine for spiritual salvation, a good marriage arrangement, or secure employment. An officiating priest (*kapurāla*) will emerge from the door of the shrine structure and offer a touch of sandal paste for the forehead or pour sacred water (*theertham*) on the hands or head of a pilgrim.

> This annual event is also a social gathering for these people; they gossip, renew their friendships (or break them, as the case may be), and generally enjoy themselves... mystics talk about their experiences, discuss spiritual matters, invent myths... Kataragama is a catalyst of social change...(Obeyesekere 1981:2).
>
> ...the most significant aspect of the festival is the passion and the sensuality, the celebration of the god's dark and illicit love life (*ibid*.:4).

Kāvadi "the joyous, exuberant dance" (*ibid*.:2) is almost painful. The dance is sacred to the deity. The arched shoulder pole, decorated with whips of tinsel, varigated paper, and peacock feathers can be seen bouncing on

---

[1] This kind of relationship is known as personal devotion to a deity (*bhakti*). It means a direct body-to-body relationship with your belief system personified in your selected shrine image.

the shoulders of ecstatic people in dance-motion (*kāvāḍi attam*). A pilgrim makes a vow to dance *kāvāḍi* around the shrine to accompanying music of horns and drums (*nageswaram*).

Fire walking comes after the occasion of the last night's formal procession (*perahāra*) in honor of the deity. The participants, as in *kāvāḍi* dance, make a religious vow to purify themselves by running, dancing, or walking over a flat bed of hot embers as a purifying act.

The Äsala season ends with the water cutting ceremony (*diya kāpīma*). At the selected auspicious minute, the forest hewn weapon of the deity is put in the stream; and a reserved pot of water is poured into the stream so that a new gathering of water can be made in the pot (*kendi*) for annual inner shrine storage.

The release of the deity's weapon (*kap*) into the stream and the pouring of water kept in the shrine is symbolic of interacting with divine entities for the maintenance of life: *water and deity* (see Raghavan 1962:66).

The scene at the *dēvāle* is crowded during festival occasions; and quiet and tranquil in the lull season. The deity shrines have existed interdependent with both Hindu and Buddhist systems in Śrī Lankā:[2]

> Kataragama [shrine] cannot be studied in isolation from the Buddhist part of the complex. The pilgrim pays the conventional homage to the deity, an offering of fruit, and then he goes to the [Buddhist stupa] Kiri Vihāra... The noise and bustle of the god's shrine is not heard here...(*ibid.*:4).

Dēvāles vary from a simple hut shrine in a Buddhist monastery to a grand edifice with a complex of buildings and grounds. But, usually a *dēvāle* consists of similar architectural features. The palace of the deity is the key structure housing the image. The design follows a South Indian pattern established during the time of the Kandyan kings. This image house (*pratimā gruha*) holds the deity's figure in the *garbha gruha* (*sancta sanctorum*, inner chamber) where only the priests enter for purification activity. Above the *garbha gruha* there is an honorific abode (*udumahal ge*) or celestial house for the divine being (as in the South Indian tradition of the *śikhara* or elevated portion of the shrine). A portico (*antarāla*) and outer platform (*maṇḍapa*) with supporting columns and roof compose the public entry space. An extended entrance corridor (*diggē*) provides a sheltered area for participating drummers and musicians.

---

[2] The motion picture *Kataragama— God for All Seasons* presents the interdependent dimensions of the belief system in Śrī Lankā.

From the *dēvāle* proper, a path or road leads to the street where processions (*perahāra*) are conducted in the town to a royal seat (*sinhāsanaya*). On the *dēvāle* grounds, a number of other shrines are located to Ganesha or Pattini, where appropriate priests (*kapurālas*) enact ritual performance. The images and *bō*-trees to the Buddha are symbolic as a *kapurāla* (priest) does not specifically attend to them. A special foods kitchen (*multānge*) and an offering storehouse (*gabaḍāgē*) are essential in terms of the *dēvāle's* wealth utilization.

The priests (*kapurālas*) usually dwell in the immediate vicinity of the *dēvāle*. Their existence is adequate; but, as religious men, they tend to spend funds on items important to functional duties. A *basnāyaka nilamē* also has an office in the premises to oversee the activities of the shrine. The role of the *basnāyaka nilamē* is to administrate the *dēvāle*.

Basnāyaka Nilamē

The name *basnāyaka nilamē* is the ancient title given to the lord or chief official of the *dēvāle* as the pivot of the supporting *rājakāriya* system. *Rājakāriya* simply means the services rendered to the *dēvāle* by the "tenants" of the *dēvāle* lands (*dēvālagam*). The system works on a land tenure basis: families are able to cultivate *dēvāle* lands by the appointment of an ancient king. In appreciation, the families maintain the *dēvāle* and participate in *grand* ritual functions. The long list of duties include providing provisions; cleaning the *dēvāle* grounds; white washing the buildings; making decorative arches; suppling coconut oil and wicks for lamps; carrying banners in procession; dancing; and bringing various foods and traditional decorum, like *betel* leaves, for the officials. One family might have the responsibility to donate roofing (paddy) straw; and another family might engage in tending to the work of thatching the *dēvāle* roof with that straw. In the festival season, the *dēvāle* is completely restored and beautified for the proceedings. The Äsala perahära is one of the largest yearly events. The *basnāyaka nilamē* is responsible to the authority of the Buddha, Kataragama Deviyo, and the state (ancient crown) for a proper and refined event for the people.

The *dēvāle* system is part of the South Indian religious/economic network (see Presler 1987). Since the time of the Sinhalese kings, the *dēvāle* has been, and continues to be, the repository for the deity as the redistributor of land and resources. The shrine is where the royal seat (*sinhāsanaya*) remains in a relationship with the polity of religion. It is the exact place in the Lévi-Straussian sense where the sacred-and-profane are seated in juxtaposition: the symbolic forms of the deity and secular government. Privilege and service are the coupled display of access and wealth at different levels for the individuals who outlay and receive things for the shrine. With such a position, the deity is richly endowed with security.

In the words of Arjun Appadurai (1981:205):

> The study is the centre of the south Indian temple [shrine]. This deity is not a mere image or icon for the expression of abstract religious sentiments and principles. In its capacity to command and redistribute economic resources, and in its capacity to rank individuals and groups, by the unequal redistribution of these resources, the deity is founded on the south Indian understanding of sovereignty.

In Badulla, there is a Kataragama shrine where the ancient *basnāyaka nilamēs* were appointed by the Sinhalese king on the basis of loyalty to the royal house. The *dēvāle* was exempt from crown taxation according to the *basnāyaka nilamē* of the *dēvāle*, Mr. Dissanayake. The British kept strict records of the people owing services and goods to the *dēvāle* as it was an official basis of land tenure. Today this ancient system of *rājakāriya* (royal service) prevails as a complete system from *dēvāle* and *basnāyaka nilamē* to land-renter and/or cultivator.

*   *   *

This following life account was recorded in the context of making a motion picture about the life of the *basnāyaka nilamē* who was elected to his post by the Ūva district revenue officers in 1980. I began this enquiry during the summer of that time with the idea to follow this official through his tenure of four years. In the summer of 1981, I again attended to the process of recording facts about the *dēvāle* chief official. I received his written life account in English and I continued to film the reconstructed events of his life account in the method I had begun with the headmonk's motion picture. The research film was made with the *basnāyaka nilamē* and the *dēvāle* members to display the annual *rājakāriya* events as well as the life account of this *dēvāle* chief.

H. B. Dissanayake 1953

Basnāyaka Ṇilamē

Name: H. B. Dissanayake

Native village: Perawella, Ūva Province

Residing village: Badulla, Ūva Province

Date of birth: June 11th, 1924

Caste: Govigama[1] (cultivators)

Time and place of record: This account was written in English by H. B.
Dissanayake in the summer of 1981 at the
Badulla Kataragama Dēvāle.

Account from the hand of H. B. Dissanayake:

*I was born on 11th of June, 1924, in the village called Perawella in the
Welimada electorate, which was a very undeveloped and backward area at
that period.*

In the summer of 1981, I retraced the past of H. B. Dissanayake by
going to his native place in the mountains of Ūva Province near the Range
of the Sleeping Soldier.

I have a sister and three brothers and I am the youngest in my family.

Being the youngest sibling makes H. B. Dissanayake the "child" of the
family. I have observed that he enjoys playing with children (his own and
others') to the point of playing big brother to them all. He is the youngest
who has succeeded to the highest position in his family.

*My father was the Rest House Keeper in Welimada, which was our
nearest town. He was a very active man with fiery looks and indomitable
strength. I am very proud of his strength and vigour that was utilized in the
welfare of the family but also the village as well. As a farmer, he devoted
his time and wealth in growing vegetables, such as beetroot, carrots, onions,
beans, tomatoes, and potatoes etc. in his own land during his leisure. Even
at this stage, I recollect with great pleasure how I extended my help in wa-
tering and nursing the vegetable plants, though yet a small kid.*

H. B. Dissanayake recounts the vegetables famous for the temperate
Ūva Province. He recalls his participation in the cultivation of the vegetables. In the motion picture, the natural essence of tending the produce in
the garden is illustrated by H. B. Dissanayake's grandson. In the scene, the

---

[1] See note 1 in chapter *Headmonk (Loku Hāmuduruvō)*.

boy tends cabbage leaves close to the ground. The careful inspection of the leaves derives from what H. B. Dissanayake said about the maintenance of the plants. This feeling has continued with H. B. Dissanayake in the course of his various occupations. It is a feeling to care for what is growing with awareness and discipline. This way to enjoy life for life's development is a Buddhist concept which is connected to the sacredness of living things; and the discipline to watch over them as a guardian.

Most of the people of Perawella were farmers who grew vegetables and paddy for their living. To sell their products they had to go to Ragala fair about four miles away from our village. There were no motorable roads and they had to carry their products either by themselves or by way of caravans. Jingling of bells of such loaded cattle moving in a line to which we called thawalama was a very pleasant and interesting scene to us. To reach this particular market place, the farmers and animals had to surpass an arduous climb of nearly four miles of steep mountainous foot paths through jungle stricken with dangerous animals, such as leopards, wild boar, and also harmless animals, such as deer, porcupine, and hare. The latter was hunted by some villagers as a recreation when they have completed cultivating their lands in autumn.

This passage tells of the pleasant views observed when the caravans made their way to the market. The difficult short journey on forest pathways was of economic necessity. People went on foot without carts. Pathways were utilized and maintained by the villagers in the area. The last sentence refers to the "harmless animals, such as deer, porcupine, and hare" (see Banks and Banks 1986). The hunting of these animals seems to be a contradiction in terms of the concept *ahiṃsā* (non-violence). The Sinhalese Buddhists have the greatest respect for nature and life. Yet these people fish the seas and streams and hunt in the forests. The answer is an economic one. The villagers exploit their natural resources to a degree. But, in their exploitation, they keep an aware balance in terms of the effects they cause to the environment. Autumn is the harvest season, and some men, usually of the lower castes, will hunt. The Sinhalese Buddhist will eat small amounts of meat. The meat is smoked, or dried, or prepared fresh. The question is a practical one for the villagers. They usually reply by saying meat in limited amounts is healthy and tastes good. The Buddhist moral question is explained in terms of the past culture. The monks claim, for instance, that the Buddha himself ate meat if it was given to him as an offering (*dāna*). The Buddha said monks could not refuse religious offerings. In terms of the villagers, they eat only modest amounts of meat as a course along with separate dishes of various vegetables. Rice remains a staple.

When I was about three years old, my father brought our whole family
to Badulla where we settled down permanently. The house where we came
into occupation is called Wataluwe Gedara, which was the ancestral property
of my father.

H. B. Dissanayake reflects on his childhood with the pleasant traditional view of a past, famous and secure, among the Sinhalese. At an
early age, H. B. Dissanayake remembers the family move from the rural
mountainous area to the town. Their house was an ancestral home in the
provincial capital: Badulla. This would be a place for academic and religious learning.

Very soon I was admitted to St. Bede's College, a Catholic school,
where I received my primary education and where my eldest brother was an
English teacher. At my father's guidance, I attended Vidyottansa Piriveṇa
on Saturdays in order to learn Pāli, the Buddha's language. Other children
of my village spent Sundays playing various games, while I was compelled to
attend Sunday school to acquire a systematic religious knowledge. I studied
my religion with great interest as this stimulated me more than the play-
ground.

This last statement is important because it illustrates H. B. Dissanayake's early Buddhist education; even though, he went to a Catholic
school. As the headmonk, he went to a Christian school for his primary
education—but, even at a young age, he went to a Buddhist college (Vidyottansa Piriveṇa) to learn Pāli. He was self motivated for learning the
traditions, yet not to become a scholar.

It is interesting that H. B. Dissanayake's elder brother was an English
teacher at St. Bede's College. During the time of British colonial rule, English was the language of administration. The college was Roman Catholic
as in the tradition of former Portugese rule (1509–1650). In a plural cultural environment where cultural boundaries are distinct, there is also the
tendency among some people to know the several traditions and languages.
These people become cross-cultural. This is the case of many educated
people in South Asia: they are multi-cultural and multi-lingual. Even in
the case of religions, some people cross from one to the next with the ability
to accept or at least to understand the values of the other.

There was a Sinhalese Literary Association in St. Bede's College. This
literary association was comprised of the grades five, six, seven and eight...I
was in grade five at this time. I remember the name of a boy in grade
eight who was proposed to be the secretary of this association. But this boy
declined the proposal and he himself proposed my name instead. This was
carried by a unanimous vote. The piriveṇa education moulded my behavior

and character to a greater extent and enabled me to be distinctive among the rest.

Already H. B. Dissanayake at an early age developed the traits of leadership by becoming an officer in the Sinhalese Literary Association at St. Bede's College. He was chosen on his ability and good honor by the boy proposed for the position. This gave H. B. Dissanayake the self-confidence and cultural reliance necessary for a person to rise in the social network.

I served as the general secretary for a full term. Besides, I must mention with gratitude that the Catholic De La Salle Brothers who taught us had a soft corner [for me] in spite of my being a Buddhist.

Again the cultural cross-over is noticed when the Catholic brothers pay particular attention to their Buddhist student.

I was appointed by the class teacher to be responsible for ringing the bell after every period and at the beginning and closing of school. The clock was facing our class and could be seen at a glance.

Here H. B. Dissanayake was given responsibility by the authority of his teacher to signal the class for recess. It seems that he was given positions which enabled him to show his ability.

It was the custom of this school to ring the bell at every half an hour and the Catholics were expected to recite a short prayer. The other children, belonging to various denominations, were silent. But as a custom, I was in the habit of silently reciting some gāthās [Buddhist verses].

In terms of reciting prayer, H. B. Dissanayake participated during the moment of prayer and recited Buddhist *gāthā* as the religious expression in the classroom.

At sixteen years of age, I was admitted to a Buddhist high school which is now called Dharmadūta Māha Vidyālaya. I urged my new class teacher to permit me to attend the Pāli class. But he did not consent to my request as he was under the opinion that Buddhism was not taught in Catholic schools on principle. As I stressed my request, I was asked to recite a stanza from Karaneeya Metta Sūtraya. The teacher was astonished that I, a pupil from a Catholic school, could recite several stanzas accurately. This resulted in my being allowed to study Pāli. Pāli Bhāshawataranaya written by Rev. Buddhadatta was the text used in the class.

Once entering the Buddhist high school Dharmadūta, he could study Pāli as a course. This persistence to learn Pāli and the literary traditions of his Buddhist culture was self-motivated. But, also as in the case of the headmonk, H. B. Dissanayake was living in an era of Buddhist revival and national consciousness. Educated people were placing a premium value on national cultural self-image and self-reliance as a positive move toward inevitable independence from the British. In the motion-picture documentation, a sequence was made of the boys at Dharmadūta High School to show H. B. Dissanayake as a student in the Buddhist college setting.

My father drew a meager salary and when I realized it was not enough to meet the family expenses, I thought of giving up my studies and doing a job.

H. B. Dissanayake knew the importance of education as his father insisted on it. But, the family economic support was also vital to their way of life. So, the youngster worked during his late teens for the household.

For one year I worked as a conductor in a tea estate. I was then completely cut off from my family, friends, and the usual surroundings. Isolated life in the tea estate was very boring to me.

One year on a tea estate is a lonely experience when the job is to oversee laborers. Usually a Sinhalese *conductor* lives separately from the Tamil (i.e., South Indian) workers, who were brought in by the British to work the estates miles away from the usual Sinhalese villages. Ūva Province is a mountainous place famous for highland tea. Many estate conductors complain about the boredom of managing tea laborers in a remote place. It seems that in the course of life, there must be a number of exciting or interesting events or happenings to make living interesting and healthy. He never elaborated on his "lonely" life on the estate, but it was another step in his experience of learning the art of management.

This happened to be the time when the Second World War began. Applications were called from those who desired to join the army. I too was ambitious to go abroad, and grasped this.

From the tea estate, H. B. Dissanayake heard the news of the war in Europe. So, he decided to take a chance in military service and travel the world. Also, I believe he was influenced by the European tea planters, who were very prominent people in the Ūva highlands.

In order to do this, I went to Colombo, where new entrants were admitted. At the army headquarters, the European gentleman (I did not know what his title was) who interviewed us questioned me as to why I wanted to join the army. I understood his mentality and answered, "To serve the British Empire." The officer smiled and seemed satisfied by my answer.

Though there were more than a hundred applicants, only four were selected, and I was included in this batch.

H. B. Dissanayake's background prepared him for his service in the British Armed Forces against Germany. In a way, H. B. Dissanayake played jokingly with the military officer to join the armed forces. But, it must be remembered that the Sinhalese people usually displayed a genuine overall sense of being a part of the greater British Empire.

After the usual three months training, we were sent to the Middle East. I had to serve in several places in Egypt. Some of them were Alexandria [Al-Iskandariyah], Cairo, Port Said, and Ismailia [Al-Ismāīlīyah]. While in Cairo, I visited the Japanese Gardens at 'Helwan', where there were a number of Buddhist statues. At this place, I felt I was at a Buddhist temple. I also visited Jerusalem and saw most of the holy places of Jesus Christ.

Again the Buddhist influence emerges in distant Cairo as H. B. Dissanayake appreciates the Buddha images in the Japanese Gardens. The holy places are of interest to him because of the Catholic school education and also because Śrī Lankā is a plural society where people of Buddhist, Hindu, Christian, and Islamic faiths worship at the famous Sinhalese shrines (e.g., Adam's Peak, or Śrī Pāda, is a religious mountain for Christians and Islamics who claim the spot for the imprint made by Adam as he ascended to heaven; or Buddhist who say that the Buddha himself touched the mountain summit; or Hindus who hold that Śiva's divine foot touched it). H. B. Dissanayake decided to make pilgrimages in the 'holy lands' of the Middle East as he would have done in Śrī Lankā.

My girl friend, who was in Ceylon [Śrī Lankā] came to my recollections very often. I wrote to her whenever I could find time.

According to expectations in Sinhalese society, a girl waits for her boyfriend. Girls are not usually allowed to go with just anyone. Usually the family, close relations, and especially the girl's brothers will make sure she has a suitable relationship and marriage proposal.

It is interesting that H. B. Dissanayake made no formal mention of an Italian girlfriend—although, privately he told me about her. In his personal photo-album, he has kept a studio photograph of the Italian friend with himself in the picture.

I experienced a new life in Egypt; and, at leisure hours, I got much satisfaction by walking through vineyards along the Nile river side.

Once, the ship in which I was travelling to Eden [Aden] was attacked by a Japanese submarine; we escaped death by a hair's breadth.

I wonder how he knew it was a Japanese submarine that attacked the ship on which he was aboard?

In Cairo, the Royal Signals Examination and proficiency in English [examination] were held, and I came in with flying colours. The result was, I was upgraded to the sergeant post after a short training.

In this section, H. B. Dissanayake again recounts the advantage he had in military service because of his education.

In 1946, I came to Ceylon [Śrī Lankā] and joined the public service as a clerk. This enabled me to take the hand of my girl friend who was waiting for me all this time. Indeed, she became a dutiful wife. She did almost every household activity, and I was set free to do social work, which gave me pleasure from childhood onwards. My partner encouraged me in this direction and watched with much delight.

Here, H. B. Dissanayake is glad to express his girl friend faithfully waited for him during his military service. After marriage, she was willing to support his public service activities as her position as wife. The role of a dutiful wife to her husband is the traditional mode of cultural performance. Mrs. Dissanayake always attended to her husband because the success of H. B. Dissanayake was vital to the livelihood of their entire family. Mutual interdependency meant a way of doing things for the family's well being.

I served five years in Badulla and later in Monarāgala, Hambegamuwa, and Wellawāya [outlying areas in Ūva Province]. All those places except Badulla were rural areas.

H. B. Dissanayake enjoyed his rural area service. But, he also missed working in the provincial center, Badulla, where he could serve on a broad basis; and where his children could receive better education.

I had the chance of coming to my home town, Badulla, again in 1952. Henceforth, I could engage in social service on a broad scale. I served as the general secretary of the Ūva Pushpadāna [flower donating] Society, a committee member of the Mutiyangana Vihāra Development Society, the general secretary of the Sasanarakshaka Madalaya, and the joint secretary of the Public Servants Buddhist Society.

These passages explain H. B. Dissanayake's commitment to public service and his wife's commitment to him and his social role. In each case, and from my own observation, Mrs. H. B. Dissanayake has supported her husband so he could fulfill obligations to maintain his leadership position.

I had the opportunity of associating with most of the nāyaka theros of the Mutiyangana Rāja Mahā Vihāra.

The Buddhist network system is very important in Sinhalese society, and awareness of that social network is a known factor. H. B. Dissanayake came in contact with many religious people during his service as a Kachcheri clerk.

At the request of the Rev. Palīpāna Chandānanda Nāyaka Thero, I served as the basnāyaka nilamē in charge of the perahāra activities.

H. B. Dissanayake was appointed as temporary *basnāyaka nilamē* by a Buddhist headmonk for a temple procession (see Seneviratne 1978).

The Hon. Governor General visited Badulla in 1968 to place the foundation stone to the YMBA building. When he visited the Mutiyangana Vihāraya, I received him at the request of the nāyaka thero [headmonk]. I must say I did this job with much pride and delight. I remember how I received him by offering betel leaves after the Sinhalese traditional custom.

This was a striking incident because, while there were higher officials, a simple peti [petty] officer was picked up by the nāyaka thero to receive the governor general.

The incident of offering betel leaves to the governor general of Śrī Lankā was of social importance for H. B. Dissanayake. Here the headmonk of the "royal" temple, Badulla, selected H. B. Dissanayake to make the honorific/symbolic present of betel leaves to the head of the state. This symbolic act, in a way, was the testing ground for the government clerk to accept higher duties.

This reminds me how I was selected to be the general secretary of the Sinhalese Literary Association while there were boys in upper classes.

Wherever I went, I could win the hearts of the society; and, also I could do any kind of job with co-operation.

Soon after the retirement, I was selected to be the basnāyaka nilamē of the Badulla Kataragama Dēvālaya [dēvāle].

No doubt the [Buddhist] pirivena education must have thrown a light on my life.

After serving as public staff clerk, 1946–1980, in ascending official capacities from rural clerk to headquarters (*kachcheri*) administrative secretary, Badulla; H. B. Dissanayake retired with the support of the district revenue officers of a higher grade who elected him *basnāyaka nilamē* in Badulla. H. B. Dissanayake claims that his training and education in the basic classical traditions of the Sinhalese culture supported his ascending stations to his high status position as chief administrator of a traditional shrine. It is said he was the first person without previous high position and wealth to attain that station.

*   *   *

Usually a man from the Kandyan aristocratic (*radala*) families will hold the position of *basnāyaka nilamē* for the Kataragama Dēvāle. But, in the years since independence, the ancient system of landlords (*nindagam*) was gradually abolished in favor of a more democratic process. By 1979, H. B. Dissanayake was able to contest, campaign, and earn high office.

Exorcist Practice

> Any firm systematization of belief would be a product of anthropological reconstruction rather than the villager's mind. From his standpoint, it is more accurate to think of various kinds of supernatural reality, more or less overlapping, more or less integrated.
>
> —Bryce Ryan 1958:106

Lankā, or Śrī Lankā, has a continuous written record of history on its civilization for about two millennia. Before the Sinhalese accounts were compiled, the name of the island was mentioned in the Sanskrit text *Rāmāyana* as the place of Ravana, who even the deities feared.

Legend, and the written chronicle *Mahāvamsa*, says the indigenous beings of Lankā were known as *dēva*, *yakkhā*, and *nāga*. Since the beginning of human recorded existence in Śrī Lankā, there was always reference to the spirits and deities. The *Mahāvamsa* expresses the situation at the time when Vijaya, the exiled prince from northern South Asia, arrived in Śrī Lankā. It seems the country was ruled and populated by *nāga* and *yakkhā*. Some scholars attribute the observation to the *fact* that darker looking forest people once inhabited the island. Those "indigenous" people sponsored cults[1] to *yakkhā* (i.e., spirits of the natural conditions of life), and *nāga*: serpents (i.e., water spirits). The *nāga* are water deities, mentioned often in Buddhist stories, residing in the seas, rivers, or on islands. Serpents—*nāga* (i.e., cobras); and of course there is a sexual connotation with the shape.

The chronicle also declares the *yakkhā* had urban states, the cultivation of rice, and the art of spinning. The indigenous people lived before the arrival of the Aryans personified in the coming of Vijaya. Prince Vijaya was exiled from North India by his father of the lion race, who wanted to punish his unruly son. Vijaya sailed with seven hundred of his men to Lankā, where he established a kingdom among the *yakkhā* and *nāga*. A queen of the *yakkhā*, a *yakkhinī*, "seduced" Vijaya by becoming a "lovely maiden" equipped with a canopied bed at the foot of a tree. The prince:

> ...took her to him as his spouse and lay with her blissfully on that bed; and all his men encamped around the tent. As the night went on, he heard the sounds of music and singing and asked the *yakkhinī*, who was lying near him, 'What means this noise?' And the *yakkhinī* thought: 'I

---

[1] See S. Paranavitana's (1929) article "Pre-Buddhist Religious Beliefs in Ceylon" for thoughts on the nature of spirits in the early belief system.

will bestow kingship on my lord; and all the *yakkhā* must be slain, for else the *yakkhā* will slay me, for it was through me that men have taken up their dwelling in Lankā.' She said to the prince: 'Here, there is a *yakkhā* city called Sirī Savatthu where a great multitude is gathered together in celebration. Even today do thou destroy the *yakkhā*, for afterwards it will no longer be possible.' He listened to her and did as she said and slew all the *yakkhā*. When he had fought victoriously, he put on the garments of the yakkhā king and bestowed on his followers. He spent some days at the spot and then went to Tambapaṇṇi. There Vijaya founded the city Tambapaṇṇi and dwelt there with the *yakkhinī*, surrounded by his ministers.

When they had founded settlements in the land, the ministers all came together and spoke to the Prince, 'Sir, consent to be consecrated as king.' But, in spite of their demand, the Prince refused the consecration, unless a maiden of noble house could be consecrated as queen at the same time.

But the ministers, whose minds were bent upon the consecrating of their lord. . .overcame all anxious fears about the matter, and sent people entrusted with many precious gifts, jewels, pearls, and so forth to the city of Madurā. . .to woo the daughter of the Paṇḍu King for their lord. . .and they also sent to woo the daughters of others for the ministers and retainers.

Vijaya had one son and one daughter by the *yakkhinī*. When he now heard the Princess had arrived, he ordered the *yakkhinī* to leave, as "men stand ever in fear of superhuman beings." The *yakkhinī* fled in terror to meet a swift death by a *yakkhā* crowd's violence. Both children were taken by the *yakkhinī's* brother to grow and multiply in the mountain forests of Sabaragamuwa as the Pulinda tribe.

Then King Vijaya consecrated the daughter of the Pandu King with solemn ceremony as his queen. He bestowed wealth on his ministers (adapted *Mahāvamsa* 1912).

When Prince Vijaya came with his followers, he brought with him the "civilizing" belief system of Brahman tradition, which overarched the indigenous beliefs. The indigenous practices and beliefs were incorporated over the centuries into the "mainstream tradition." In Southeast Asia this occurred as in Thailand:

Thai religious complexity is of the sort commonly characterized as syncretic, in which elements derived from several historically discrete traditions have combined to form a single distinctive tradition. In such a situation, individuals may simultaneously hold beliefs or practice rituals derived from different traditions, without any apparent sense of incongruity (Kirsch 1977:241).

The nation of Sinhalese emerged by the conquest of the so called "indigenous beings." The acculturation process was severe to those people who were not in the mainstream of the Aryan settlers (Maloney 1974a:128).

When Buddhism arrived at Śrī Lankā in the 3rd Century B.C., the faith became the new arch over incongruent constituents (Paranavitana 1929). Each constituent of the belief system had a part and responsibility to the center: the Buddhist king. The approaches for understanding a social syncretic situation are numerous. The Sinhalese belief system is a manifestation of a multi-dimension cognitive construct, which states people recognize themselves to *be* as a nation. No matter how the belief system is *cut*, in my study it is treated as a contemporary entity: founded, transformed, and maintained by the Sinhalese people.

Supernatural Beings

Bryce Ryan (1958) explains about the six types of "supernatural" powers active in village life in his *Sinhalese Village*:

> Although these powers are not hierarchically graded, the Buddha stands above all others...especially Vishnu, and Kataragama (the Sinhalese version of Skanda), and Saman, a distinctively Sinhalese deity, and a host of associated dēvas (*ibid.*:106).

The pantheon categories continue:

> All of these are considered part of Sinhalese culture with no conscious recognition of their affiliations with Hinduism. In a third category, distinct from the Hindu type pantheon, are the planet gods influencing every phase of the individual's life (*ibid.*).

The planetary deities could cause disease and are utilized for predicting the future in horoscope devices, but the intervening spirits are...

> Utterly apart from planet gods, but affiliated with the pantheon of dēvas are the *yakas* [i.e., *yakkhā*] or demons and with them a multitude of wood spirits [i.e., small or elusive supernatural beings], and ghosts. Loosely associated with the demon world is a realm of diffuse supernatural power less explicitly attributable to particular entities, e.g. auspicious meetings, evil mouth, the plethora of charms, and rituals...(*ibid.*:106–107).

Another and last "supernatural realm" is sorcery or black magic.

Although black magic operated through a specific demon, it is so systematized that we should view it as a distinct type (*ibid.*:107).

The Sinhalese have a vast array of supernatural beings in their pantheon. A village area is one abstraction of the vast South Asian system of beliefs that seem to defy precise definition.

McKim Marriott found that in a village in the Doab of the Ganga plains there were 90 deities. These, he said could be divided into three levels. Of them, 30 were recognizable as gods of the great pantheon, whereas 60 had not been integrated into the Sanskritic tradition. Of these 60, a dozen were regional deities mentioned in Hindi literature as having important cults and temples (Maloney 1974a:171).

This is a revised list (based on the record of Paul Wirz, 1954:23-24) of "evil" beings in Sinhalese culture which inhabit the four worlds:

600,000	garuda-yakku,
10,000	asura-yakku,
80,000	brāhmaṇa-yakku,
20,000	vetali-yakku,
20,000	mahipāla-bahirava-yakku,
40,000	rākshasa,
20,000,000	bhūta,
100,000,000	preta,
90,000,000	pisāca.

From the provinces of South Asia, the system and the participating principle deities are slightly redefined from the religious entities of Buddhism, Hinduism, Jainism, Islam, Christianity, and isolated forest cults (see Seligmann *et al.* 1911). But the diverse elements of spirit-beings are arranged in a defined network. In Śrī Lankā, the belief system includes a spirit pantheon under the "trusteeship" of guardian deities. The spirits are usually evil and unjust, according to the Sinhalese. Only specialists can interact and understand the nature of spirits in a village.

Myth

The *tovil* is a Sinhalese performance of exorcism. The act is conducted by a professional exorcist, *yakādurā* or *gurunnānse*, who dances or/and chants *mantra* (e.g., South Asian oral formulas for expelling evil) in order to dispel evil spirits from a person's body.[2]

---

[2]   Paul Wirz (1954) has the most complete ethnography of the *yak tovil* in his

The Sanni Yakuma *tovil* ceremony is one of the most famous among the Sinhalese. Sanni Yakuma is the generic name assigned to a group of eighteen evil spirits of disease which are Bhūta, Abhuta, Maru, Amukku, Vedi, Vāta, Pit, Ginijal, Gulma, Jala, Bihiri, Kana, Golu, Sitala, Deva, Mṛtu, Demala, and Kola. Each spirit represents a specific illness in the Sinhalese health system.

The story of the spirits' origin has been passed along the generations. Sankhapāla, a king of Lichchavi, was living with his queen, Asūpāla, when the king was called away to war. The queen was pregnant at the time with the king's child; but, the king was not aware of this fact. While the king was away, the queen had a desire for a variety of mango called *mī-amba*. As the fruit was not in season, the ministers had to search to find one fruit. A female servant heard of the fruit's arrival, and also wanted a taste. When the servant observed the queen eating the fruit, she asked the queen for a piece. But the queen refused, saying that one fruit could not be shared. Angered by the refusal, the servant girl decided to take revenge on the queen. So, when the king returned from his war victory, the servant secretly told the king the queen was carrying a child from a union with a minister. The king was enraged by the report and ordered the queen be taken to cemetery where an axeman was ordered to cut her in half. The unborn prince protected himself in one side of the queen's deposed body. After a passage of ten months, the prince re-formed himself into a young man and nourished himself with the human remains in the cemetery. He soon commanded a group of eighteen spirits.

By the divine force of deity Iśwara, the flesh eating prince was given a memory of previous existences; and, he came to know of how his innocent mother died. So, he decided to take revenge with his retinue on his father's kingdom. The attack was brutal; and, the city was wasted. Disease and famine spread throughout the land. The Buddha heard of the revengeful act and visited the area from his monastery in Jetawana. The great sage recited the *Ratana Sutta* (Gem Sayings) and asked that the evil spirits be served with an offering of rice in a leaf bowl. With that gesture, order was restored to humans. But, the spirits lived in the forests and inauspicious spaces (e.g., cemeteries or cross-roads), and manifested themselves as illnesses to people. The Buddha commissioned the deities Nātha and Saman (guardian deity of Śrī Pāda) to oversee the activities of the spirits.

---

chapter entitled "The Sanniya-Yakuma-Ceremony" of *Exorcism and the Art of Healing in Ceylon.*

Ritual

The act of exorcism is the interaction between the exorcist and the illness causing spirit. Special preparations are made for the ceremony. A shed (i.e., spirit's palace) is crafted of banana-tree stems and coconut leaves. An offering of flowers, selected sweet meats, and betel nut is placed on the shed's alter. The spirits are invoked by the representation of themselves in the dance (i.e., exorcism) so they will partake the offerings.

The Sanni dance (i.e., *tovil*) is acted out from sunset to sunrise in the prescribed area in front of the patient. The patient's relations are present nearby and close to the patient. Other villagers are in the perimeter observing, joking, and playing cards as the performance goes on (Kapferer 1975).

During the first watch of the evening (*sändäsamayama*), the first of the performers in the guise of an evil spirit comes on the "stage" area to dance. Each evil spirit only knows a part of the universe and is a specialist in only one kind of illness. So, the exorcist invokes them according to his need to arrest the illness. The night or mid-night watch (*mahāsamayama*) is the height of the performance in terms of evil presence. Then, the morning watch (*aluyama samayama*) comes and the dancers act the various roles of the spirits. By dawn, the exhausted dancers perform for a sleepy audience. The resting patient, kept awake during the night, is fatigued. The last dance is the appearance of the beautiful unifying deity who wears all the evil spirits suppressed in his crown (i.e., headdress). Only the deity can solve the illness and re-collect the patient as a whole person after the spirits have glanced at themselves, partaken of the offering, and fled from the demarcated space. The patient, then, might rise from the spot and bite the head of a rooster and spit the blood sanctioned by ritual. People then disperse. The utensils, made especially for the exorcism, are thrown away. The performers go home to sleep; and, the patient should rest and recover.

Although many spirits are in the realm of the Sinhalese belief system, only a few are distinctive and popular in each village.

My intention is to illustrate the coherence of such a belief system. I will proceed to identify the Sinhalese belief system as a Buddhist—Brahmanic/Hindu—indigenous constellation: as I hold that some discrete tendencies exist in the three proportions. I have experienced the elements on three levels which range in a culturally believed hierarchy, not a social stratification. Although positive and negative social stratification exist in the form of the caste system, it is not as strong among the Sinhalese as it occurs in a pure Hindu context. The cultural belief hierarchy is a display configuration to prompt the Buddha, or pure Buddhist ideals, at the axis.

Then, there is a gradual shift into the so-called non-Buddhist elements, like Brahmanic deity or spirit distinctions. The various belief constituents exist as discrete integrated levels or processes. The individual components infinit; but, I find they cluster into several major heuristic tendencies.

There is no heresy under the name of a Buddhist hero if the heterogeneous elements close the hiatus of antagonism and become part of one moral system. The Buddhist—non-Buddhist dilemma in the Sinhalese belief system is a question of "pure" or "impure" levels of Sinhalese identification. This structural standard defines intersocial/personal *relationships*. Scholars can emphasize dualism as togetherness or separateness, "purity and danger," precept and practice, Buddhist and non-Buddhist, or people of the land and people not of the land, and so on. But the question is, as far as I am concerned, what emphasis is placed on the structure of the belief system vis-a-vis the individual component? The integrated elements of various persuasions (heterodoxy) finally will influence the basic individual. The individual is the basic unit which integrates into a life support system of belief.

The role of a *gurunnānse* is not a highly respected position because of its lower caste status. People associated with the arts and crafts have not been afforded a respected status until recently. Presently, public schools have established dance and craft-arts as courses in the educational process. Villages and towns currently sponsor dance performances that cut across caste lines. In the process of public performance, dance has become more a cultural form than a caste form; and thus, dance forms and the dancers are respected more across the culture.

*   *   *

The following account of a *gurunnānse* (exorcist) comes from my field study of the summer 1981. I went with Conrad Ranawake to the village area called Akurugoda in the tropical Southern Province of Śrī Lankā. Akurugoda is a rural rice growing community located about seven miles away from Mātara on the southern coast.

The rural communities of the south maintain life on the harvest of rice and on commercial rubber, cinnamon, and coconut resources. Along the coast, people fish for a living in outriggers similar to those used among Pacific Ocean island cultures (see Lambrecht 1975:13–19).

Peemachchari Nakathige Sirineris 1981

Gurunnānse

Name: Peemachchari Nakathige Sirineris (Henegama Gurunnānse)

Native village: Henegama, Southern Province

Residing village: Akurugoda, Southern Province

Date of birth: June 9th, 1930

Caste: Beravā[1] (drummers)

Time and place of record: This account was spoken in Sinhala by Peemachchari Nakathige Sirineris at his residence in mid-July 1981.

Account by Peemachchari Nakathige Sirineris:

The *gurunnānse* begins his life account with the memory of leaving school at about the age of twelve.

After leaving school around 1942, I was able to learn dancing with the help of my uncle (Edo Gurunnānse), who lived at Kōdāgoda village (nearby village). It was some kind of training. Afterward, I was able to learn more from H. N. Siyadoris Gurunnānse, who was treated as my teacher.

The *gurunnānse's* formal education was brief as he only achieved the third standard at the Henegama junior-school. He gave up school education because of the *yak tovil* ceremonies, which he attended with his father. Of course, it was difficult to attend school classes after participating in rituals over night.

Meanwhile, I learned to become popular in false leg walking (boru kakul kāraya). I enjoyed this activity. But my parents were against it. Therefore, I had to avoid it. But I still remember one story related to this activity.

One person was walking with false legs at a procession conducted in the village school. He walked up to a certain point and, unfortunately, one leg went into an unseen hole. Immediately, he fell down and broke his leg. It

---

[1] The *beravā* caste is treated as a very low caste according to the caste hierarchy. The *govigama* (cultivators) caste is the most dominant caste in Śrī Lankā. A village should have at least two families of *beravā* caste. *Govigama* caste people treat them in a separate style, never eating or drinking with them. *Govigama* people never give them high-level seats. Special cups are used for *beravā* caste people, and so on. They attend social festivals to provide the drumming for cultural processions.

was a difficult situation for this particular person. People become afraid of this situation. He recovered after three months. Even though this happened, I was not discouraged by the accident. Parents and other adults wanted me to become famous or a talented artist/dancer. They all assisted me in this line to learn dancing and the arts. Even my two eldest brothers helped me. They are P. N. Saraneris and P. N. Gimoneris. They expected me to become more popular and talented. I appreciated their assistance, and gained talents through this inheritance.

As a boy, he expresses his desire to practice walking on stilts for fairs and carnivals. The related story of the man who broke his leg is one of the detailed sequences framed in the life account. I am sure that if I asked the *gurunnānse* to expand on each aspect of his life, he would remember several detailed stories. The headmonk told me a number of stories after telling me his life account for many months. These additional stories were included in the motion picture. But, with less time to share with the *gurunnānse*, the stories were basically "primal" in the way they flowed from his recollection.

The *gurunnānse* was thankful to his brothers who had faith in him and assisted him towards the higher performance arts. His "talents through inheritance" meant that talent came directly from his family.

I am the third member of a family of nine. When I was attending school, I participated in several school ceremonies; and, at the term-end dramas which provided various types of dancing, I became popular among the villagers as well. They appreciated my performance.

The *gurunnānse* remembers he was good at giving performances for class activities in the third standard at school. Usually a school provides a chance for students to perform in the cultural events staged with the school. The events usually follow various styles of Sinhalese traditional dance. Those are the dances the *gurunnānse* presently teaches his students in front of his home. The cultural dramas are usually plays about popular stories depicting traditional life or ancient episodes of a Sinhalese royal family. The plays are popular among village folk as a diversion from daily routine: entertainment (see Sarathchandra 1953, and Goonatileka 1976).

At this moment, I would like to thank Edo Gurunnānse for his help in my training. In this way, I engaged in this field and became popular. After receiving training from Edo Gurunnānse, I returned to my parents' place, joined their team, and became a partner. Then I managed to compete with other artists of Ruhunu area.

The *gurunnānse* would like to thank his teacher Edo Gurunnānse in writing and the motion picture about his activities. In the life account, both the headmonk and the *basnāyaka nilamē* acknowledged people responsible for their success. As mentioned, the influence of the researcher and the methodological approach giving the goals and uses of the material guides the kind of information presented by the participant.

It is of interest to note that the *gurunnānse* had a special teacher who trained him in the arts rather than his family doing so. I think this was due to Edo Gurunnānse's sincere interest in the boy. Very often, in South Asia, exorcist teachers will collect an informal following of talented students, who later assist the teacher in the craft.

After training with a professional teacher, the boy returned to the family's team. As a partner in the home group, the *gurunnānse* competed at cultural events in the region of Ruhunu, east of Henegama in the Southern Province. Nur Yalman (1964) gave a detailed study in his article "The Structure of Sinhalese Healing Rituals" concerning the dances and healing rituals specific to that area; also see M. D. Raghavan's chapter "The Ruhunu Dances" (1962:98–109).

In 1947, I had a dispute with my mother and ran away from home. This helped me reach the Akurugoda area, where we find a number of excellent artists (among the numerous beravā caste families). It [the art] was more popular than in the Henegama area. Apart from all the artists of Akurugoda, H. N. Hinniyas was very popular during this time. Hinniyas Gurunnānse was more concerned with 'mantra' than with dancing.

The dispute with the *gurunnānse*'s mother was a personality conflict. It seems his mother was too strict with him—so he "ran away" to a nearby village called Akurugoda. In that village, he found many families of his own caste. The principal exorcist in the village took the *gurunnānse* as a student and assistant. Henegama is a place where many well-known exorcists originate. This was probably the reason why the *gurunnānse* chose the place to continue learning and practicing his craft. Certainly Conrad Ranawake selected Henegama as a research village for this study by the virtue of its art fame. His new teacher, Hinniyas Gurunnānse, was a specialist in *mantra* verse[2] (i.e., South Asian art of chanting spells to expel evil spirits). Here is a *mantra* for "one hundred and eight repetitions" to disarm the child influencing spirit Grahaniya-yakkini:

Om ring! Grahaniya-yakshani
(Honor to the spirit's name.)

---

[2] See S. J. Tambiah (1968) "Magical Power of Words."

Palen [Tamil] [or *palayan* (Sinhalese)]! *Dosvaha!*
(Go!)   (We hope it may be good!)
                                         (see Wirz 1954:217)

This particular guru had six children (two males and four females). One son is called Siripala (who became an exorcist); the other son is H. S. Gunatilaka (who became an artist). This is the place where I arrived. I settled down after running away.

The *gurunnānse* seemed to like his new environment. Also, his relative lived in the village area.

Hinniyas Guru also considered my situation and asked me to stay with him. So I did and attended ceremonies. After a short period, they brought me a marriage proposal, and I agreed. One of the youngest daughters of Hinniyas was selected as my partner. Her name was H. Somawathi. Our marriage took place around 1948.

The marriage proposal was conducted by Hinniyas Gurunnānse's family. The young man (the *gurunnānse*) had seen the girl earlier when he was attending a ceremony. He accepted the idea to take her as his wife. The marriage took place at the bride's home. It was performed without any difficulty. I am not sure about the attendance of the *gurunnānse's* family. Even his memory of the date was not exact. The ceremony was simple. Afterwards, he lived with his wife's family—although usually the wife should live with the husband's family until the couple are able to afford some land and a house.

The *gurunnānse* attended exorcism ceremonies with his new brother-in-law. After a year, he constructed a home in the village on his wife's family's land.

We lived at Akurugoda for a short period and went back to Henegama. Once again we had to come back to Akurugoda. We returned because of my wife's pregnancy.

The newly married couple went to the *gurunnānse's* village. But, their stay was abbreviated due to a continued conflict between the *gurunnānse* and his mother. The couple returned to the wife's village for the delivery and care of their first child.

In March 1949, we received the first baby, a son, as we expected. So, we were very happy. We named him Leelānanda. At this stage, I was a teacher of two students.

According to South Asian concepts, the first child is expected to be male. A boy represents the masculine strength of the family, he is an economic resource in terms of eventually earning a living, he carries on the name of the family, and he cares for his aged parents. Daughters are also respected among families as the Sinhalese belief system maintains a high moral regard for all persons. But, boys receive a little more preference according to the traditional model.

The fact that the *gurunnānse* expected a son was a combination of "traditional expectations" and a prediction given by a fortuneteller (as usually a newly married couple will consult an expert to observe the future).

The *gurunnānse* obtained two students for training and assistance of his own, which meant he finally achieved the status of a *gurunnānse*: teacher.

My favorite activities were (1) training of students for dancing, (2) carving masks, and (3) gokkola kalāwa — artistic work of folding palm leaves.

Continuous work related to these fields seems to be boring, and I planned to study architecture. So with one of my companions, I went to the Kandy area to learn architecture. While receiving just an introductory knowledge, I thought of coming back to Akurugoda. So I returned home [to Akurugoda].

The *gurunnānse* continued to practice the crafts mentioned. In the motion-picture account, there are scenes of mask carving and of training students to dance. I did not illustrate his journey to the Kandy region to study architecture; although the event is mentioned in the audio. I selected visual sequences with the *gurunnānse* that were relevant to his village area (near Akurugoda).

The motivation to leave home was similar to that of the headmonk and the *basnāyaka nilamē*. When the headmonk was a boy, he ran away from home to a jungle area in the north (Nikaveratiya) due to boredom with the routine of studies. The *basnāyaka nilamē* decided to join the military service and travel because he was tired of the isolation and routine of tea estate duties. According to this small sample of a few individuals, it seems that in each case, a shift or a transition occurred in their daily lives because a "change" was necessary to alter the routine. Sometimes the change is transient (e.g., the *gurunnānse*) as to another task or place that might seem better or unusual enough to sustain interest for awhile. In other cases (e.g., the headmonk) the change might lead to thoughts which eventually become a "turning" point in life (see Mandelbaum 1973).

The *gurunnānse* never successfully completed his training in architecture as he found traditional dance and exorcism to be equal, if not more worthwhile, to him as a career.

During this time, I worked helping masons and others (because of my training in architecture). But my friends, relations and other village people requested me to proceed with my traditional career—śanthi karma' [i.e., simple kind of health ceremony utilizing lime branches, which serves the people who have various minor problems]. Villagers need this service. Someone has to do it. These requests helped me work as an exorcist once again. So many types of services are being rendered:

(1) 'ādurukan'—one of the preliminary activities done to any patient for fever or headache. A family consults me. I visit the particular household and chant with coconut oil, of which I apply to the forehead of the patient or chant with a small piece of thread and tie it to the patient's arm,

(2) 'mātirili'—chant with a branch of tea or mango leaves—the patient should be kept nearby,

(3) 'dehi kāpeema'—the ritual cutting of lime to cure a patient,

(4) 'pidēni'—the offering to the yakkhā (spirits),

(5) 'tovil'—different types of yakkha exorcist ceremonies.

I was able to become a good dancer (of the low country style). In addition to tovil work, I attended a number of competitions (for low country dances).

The task lessons from his brief encounter with architecture allowed him to find additional employment assisting masons and carpenters. Again his services as an exorcist were requested for the community.

He was requested to perform simple ceremonies at first. In them, the exorcist visits the patient and chants a *mantra* while applying oil on the patient (while an oil lamp is kept burning in the room). The *gurunnānse* lists and explains five other ceremonies of his profession. It was included in the life account to inform me of his particular activities.

In 1964, the Arts Council of Ceylon conducted a competition for low country dancing, singing, and vocalizing. I was able to come first in this particular competition. I received this award performing 'dekona vilakku nātuma' (a dance where two torches burning at both ends are placed in the mouth while the person is dancing). I gained certificates for these activities. Afterwards, I attended such competitions for three years continuously; and, I gained a shield from the Arts Council.

The Arts Council of Ceylon was first established in 1952. Its objective was to carry out various programs in the fields of traditional arts. Regular festivals were conducted for the display of music, dance, drama, handicrafts, painting, drawing, sculpture, and other popular arts (Bandara 1972:20–21):

> The idea of an Arts Council for Ceylon was, no doubt, taken from the Arts Council of Great Britain,...to take account of social conditions which differ widely from those in Great Britain. In Ceylon, it may well be that the average town dweller is more ignorant of the national culture than is the villager. If so, one of the main tasks of the Council would be to revive the dormant and neglected culture of the villages themselves, rather than to take the culture of the towns to the villages.

> The Act of Parliament (Act No. 18 of 1952) which incorporated the Arts Council expanded this idea and specified the Council's objects as follows: (a) to develop a greater knowledge, understanding and practice of the fine arts; (b) to increase the accessibility of works of art to the public in Ceylon; (c) to improve the standards of execution in the fine arts; (d) to preserve, promote and encourage the development of such arts and crafts as are indigenous to Ceylon; and (e) to advise and co-operate with Government Departments, local authorities and other bodies on any matter concerned directly or indirectly with the aforesaid objectives.

> The Arts Council has carried out various programmes of work for the promotion of creative activities among artists. It has held regular festivals of music, dance and drama, exhibitions of handicrafts, painting and sculpture, published several journals and books on the arts and maintained Colombo's most popular theatre.

The *gurunnānse* participated in the Arts Council of Ceylon events for dance style, technique, and form. Some of his dances are included in the film scenes. The gestures and postures while dancing are the most difficult tasks resulting in an ecstatic performance (see Turner 1982).

In addition, I won six gold medals, one silver cup, and nearly eighteen certificates.

At the *gurunnānse's* home, I was shown the medals and certificates. He wears the six gold medals on a red sash as items for his dance costume.

As time goes on, I became old and, as a result, I spend much time in training more students and doing some minor activities related to exorcism. I lead the way and my team members or students perform everything.

As the headmonk, the *gurunnānse* explains he teaches by example rather than by strict orders. The discipline is kept arranged according to the tradition, and his way is to simply perform for interested students to observe. The motivated students take hold of the style and match it with similar determination.

But if necessary I perform dances too. At this moment, I have become a loving teacher of so many low country artists.

Already I have started a program to train local artists for dancing, singing, and playing instruments (e.g., drums). About 25–30 female students attend my classes to learn various types of dances:

(1) kulu nätum — dance using winnowing baskets,

(2) lee keli — dance using sticks,

(3) mal nätuma — dance using flowers,

(4) kalageḍi nätuma — dance using pots,

(5) and playing instruments such as the drums.

The *gurunnānse* lists the dances he instructs to a group of female students. The girls are of various ages and they dance in their own age groups. A drummer comes to accompany them at dance time. The dances mentioned appear in the motion-picture account. The dance classes have become the *gurunnānse's* regular activity and source of income.

I have worked to maintain the country's culture.

As the headmonk and *basnāyaka nilamē* have both expressed their participation in the welfare of the society's culture—the *gurunnānse* also participates for the benefit of the tradition. He maintains his art-craft for future Sinhalese to learn, practice, and perform.

There is so much evidence to prove the power of exorcism. But, today it is becoming weak. I can trace the fact for this change.

People who do not know properly (the art of the exorcist), perform these activities for commercial purposes. They have little knowledge. But it [when done properly] has power.

As I have witnessed and heard from Sinhalese colleagues, the art forms, in terms of healing and entertainment, are waning because of commercial developments in rural areas. Today the tradition is popularized as a commercial and political tool—and the artists who sincerely perform their craft suffer from the misbehavior of those who perform by commercial motivation.

The *gurunnānse* is concerned with the maintenance of his tradition. He wants to forward the discipline and pure quality in his art—as the power of exorcism depends on the quality and behavior of the performers. Exorcism is an aspect of the Sinhalese Buddhist moral system manifesting South Asian knowledge, craft, and discipline.

The practice of the exorcist is true and correct. My capability can be known through my performances. There are exorcists who do not know anything properly. These people damage our field.

"The practice of the exorcist is true and correct" is the summing-up of the *gurunnānse*. From the belief, the art of the exorcist is expressed to be as "true" as the tradition and "correct" in the discipline of the Buddhist system. The disciplines of Buddhism are multi-relationships working with order, management, morality, and faith to compose a system.

Sinhalese Belief System on Health

Belief System Dimensions

The foundation of any society is the weaving of people together.

—Gary McGill 1982

Institutions[1] preserve the status quo, therefore a standard is achieved. This conservative measure of an institution is appreciated by the participants of this research because they are part of a resilient cultural continuum. The traditional individuals of this study have a sense of place in the process of a life pattern that is interconnected regardless of specific task role, and they belong to a system intact and conservative by its nature. The participants act to preserve the entire traditional system. I never heard the research participants condemn or disregard the various aspects of a belief system. The headmonk spoke of his own way of life in the *saṅgha* as the disciplined life passage. But, he also qualified his thoughts by saying that laymen and specific others in the popular tradition lived according to valuable utility roles in the society. When I asked the headmonk about the act of pilgrimage in Śrī Laṅkā, he responded by saying people journey to visit the shrines in order to enjoy a non-routine pace of life. As daily activities are broken or suspended for the individual or group journey, people have relief from usual tasks. The pilgrimage is rough, but soothing. The people are mixed together in the comfort of the greater tradition.

The societal interaction between monk, shrine-official, and exorcist will be examined in the following pages. There is a symbolic pattern that "nets" the belief system paths together as a unity, yet these participants seldom, if ever, come into direct daily life. As most of the Śrī Laṅkā state leaders have been working to restore and maintain the traditions of the society, these three religious men have always integrated at their own levels across the social system. Private organizations such as the Young Men's Buddhist Association and the Mahā Bodhi Society have contributed to the welfare of the country's heritage. In each case, the symbols and expressions are utilized to tie the laity and religious specialists into a mainstream of culture.

Here I will give a brief list of the modes of expression which act as cultural unifiers regardless of personal activity. These elements are agreed upon by the Sinhalese at large to be obvious traditional markers, such as:

---

[1] I will use the concept of institution to mean the formal process in which people find social identity, security, and patterns for interaction as a "charter structure" for human organization based on a continuum of recognized authority.

(1) Personal Meditation

(2) Pilgrimage

(3) Healing and Entertainment (Ritual Performance)

Just from the recorded life accounts (and especially from the motion pictures) the symbolic connections were evident for the unity and sanctity of the belief system (see Douglas 1970, Turner 1977, Appadurai 1981, MacAloon 1981, C. Farber 1983, Obeyesekere 1984). As a symbolic reference, the natural environment of Śrī Lankā as a secured tropical island under the influence of the Asiatic monsoon wind system is a typical point. Sinhalese "love" their "rich," "tropical," "resplendent" island of mountains and plains. Every variation of plant life is expressed with delight. The very environment has become an artifact associated with the Sinhalese. Even the shape of the island which has been expressed in terms of a pearl, tear, or mango (or a ham shank by the Dutch) is a symbolic design which appears on state corporation signs and Vesak (Buddha's birth, enlightenment, and *parinibbāna* anniversary) cards. The Sinhalese strongly identify with the features of the island: it seems the island is positive space and the surrounding ocean is negative space.

The traditional symbols are really obvious, but they are also subliminal and partially unconscious. The symbol of the lotus is seen everywhere in Śrī Lankā, just as the rosette is a standard in the West. But, the iconic form is not always cognized, nor understood to popular tradition. Or perhaps the lotus and the rose are just beauty marks for ornamentation in public places.

Regardless of apparent usefulness, the symbols, expressions, and practices are employed as *devices* by institutional craftsmen or religious professionals. Here I will discuss the use of traditional institutional tools which are standards for cultural participation. The cases will be drawn from each life account as a cross-reference.

Mental Devices

Jacques Maquet states there are four basic modes of consciousness: first, active and volitive; second, cognitive; third, affective/emotional/feeling; fourth, contemplative. The first three belong to the affective waking state, and the fourth is a kind of peaceful "inward" conscious meditation. According to Maquet, for an aesthetic experience, the contemplative state should be employed to "observe" and "feel" the object in question. In a state of contemplation, meanings appear intuitively because the intellectual conceptualization tools are heightened for insight. The contemplative state is a prime mental device.

In terms of daily life, the difficulty is how to be in a contemplative state and cognize "facts" or "meanings" to be used in a conceptualizing language which is in another frame of consciousness. The human states of consciousness are simply mental states that vary in degree according to the context of psychological or cultural established norms. People suffering from extreme mental states are spoken of as being "possessed," in "trance," or having an induced "medicinal" experience.[2] These mental conditions extend to the levels of classified "insanity" (see Prince 1974). Different conscious states "account for the individual's altered behavior as well as for his altered subjective experience of himself and of the world" (Bourguignon 1973:3). Strange human alteration of behavior, speech, and stated goals-of-life are the classifying indicators for a "spiritually influenced" or "psychologically ill" person. People everywhere are subject to "altered states" because all humans live in multi-dimensional psychological conditions that change by a simple "mental switch." The various human altered states are utilized for various styles of thought and experience.

Different states of awareness are manifest on a continuum ranging in degree and intensity. Roland Fisher (1970) has pointed out that different conscious states have a neurophysiological basis on three planes: first, arousal of the central nervous system "ergotropic excitation"; second, the perception state ("normophrenic") of every day working activities; and third, the reduced (hypo-) arousal ranging from relaxation to meditation. Other scientists have devised classification systems to isolate conditions of conscious awareness. Arnold Ludwig (1968) has offered five variables based on sensitivity and alteredness (e.g., body motor activity, alertness, and "somatopsychological factors"). The point about every kind of classification is that there are neurophysiological underpinnings which make them cross-cultural or universal: a standard human measure. The classifications share changes, modes of thought, various time-senses, loss of control, perceptual disturbance, self image, and so on. This is to say, the position of altered states has a psychobiological/scientific standing related to every human experience. On the cultural level, contexts and meanings arrive to influence the pattern of altered states. As the human/personal condition becomes transferred to a cultural/institutional structure, mental utilization or commitment becomes apparent.

> We must note the cultural context in which the observed event occurs. Only in this way can we discover whether we are, in fact, dealing with an individual, private, perhaps deviant event or a patterned and

---

[2] For works concerning *possession, trance, medicinal experience*, and *mysticism* see Simons 1973, Stace 1973, Lewis 1978, Sharon 1978, Peters 1981, and Karim 1990; and, for Sinhalese folk ideas see Ratanapala 1991.

institutional one; whether we are dealing with a profane or secular phenomenon, one that is positively evaluated and desired or one that is negatively evaluated and feared. Only by inquiry can we discover its meaning to participants (Bourguignon 1973:13).

As I view different states of awareness as a complete relationship operating as mental content and culture, the act of meditation (i.e., "hypoarousal" in terms of Roland Fisher's classification as a continuum of altered states) is presented among the Sinhalese as an integral part of the culturally constituted behavior of the Buddhist monastic community. Jacques Maquet wrote "Expressive Space and Theravāda Values: A Meditation Monastery in Śrī Lankā" to illustrate the notion of congruence between the state of meditation and the institutional space-design to accommodate a valued condition in society. The study was important to show that first, the Sinhalese people provide specific space for an intentional meditative state different from the usual everyday-life consciousness; and second, the people's traditions have refined the appropriate utilization of meditation to *search* for personal and religious goals (e.g., a composed human nature on the way to *nibbāna*). Of course, psychological space is a human need at every level of awareness, but the Sinhalese specify more clearly the areas of traditional participation in a culturally demarcated zone. John Welwood has written about three kinds of space: the perceptual to the external world, the conceptual to abstract-notions of physics; and third, open to...

> the wide open spaces of unexplored lands, the rolling space of the restless seas, and the vast reaches of outer space, to the 'expansion' of consciousness itself, could be seen as a longing for this free open space at the very basis of our being (1977:105).

Sinhalese Buddhist psychology recognizes the deep-seated human need for open mental space in the meditation practice. Opening the mind in this way requires a specific environment for the endeavor. As stated in Maquet's article, the isolation cubicles for meditation facilitated absolute-self in a tiny world of oneself: the pivot-point of awareness. The monks and laity practicing meditation in the monastery, "open" themselves in Sinhalese cultural sanctuary.

In the unusual "isolated tradition," wandering monks (*tāpasa bhikkhu*) of the forest remove themselves from society for the *ideal* reasons of meditation for self awareness: eventual salvation. Nur Yalman (1962:315) wrote:

> ...The trappists, the Whirling Dervishes of Islam, and the ascetic hermits and wanderers of India and Ceylon, with all the varieties of doctrinal differences between them, are attempting to devise means of approaching the threshold between men and gods.

Meditation works as such a vehicle to approach a universal human attitude without prejudice. A person must be in the proper frame of mind (i.e., mind-ease) for self-resolution in time and space.

Roger Walsh (1977:152) states that scientists are making repeated requests for individuals in the behavioral sciences to explore the human consciousness as trained participant observers (Tart 1975, Globus 1976). For example, there is little in the way of reports on the initial meditative experience. Charles T. Tart (1975) goes on to say the West has studied the basic concepts of the East, such as meditation, the concept of *saṃsāra*, illusion (*māyā*) or worldly noise in far more detail than those traditions which originated the ideas. And, it seems that Western scientists do not apply the ideas to themselves. "They [scientists] assume...their own [systems] are basically logical and clear. Western psychology now has a challenge to recognize...that our 'normal' state is a state of *saṃsāra* and to apply the immense power of science and our other spiritual traditions, East and West, to the search of our way out" (*ibid.*:286).

The culture is a context for the mind dialogue. The perceptual interaction of mental abilities and culture defines the individual's pathology. The imagination of the mind is creative if the culture deems the dream to be a creative process. The question is, how far do humans go in constructing reality from the world instead of simply becoming self empty. Meditation is a way to enter into a complete introspective reflection and conscious arrangement of experience. The intentional mental and physical process is a kind of growth in terms of general well being and perceptual awareness.

Meditation is a grammar for self healing within the discipline and training of the religious experts (e.g., monks) who know the strategy of sitting to enter the self/universal frame. Buddhist psychology recognizes the methods for entering "the deeper primordial spaciousness" beneath what is generally considered to be the conditioned reality of affective (waking) space. As in the statements of Berger and Luckmann (1967), the world is created. In Buddhism, practitioners of meditation establish a rootedness by intentional concentration to connect with centerless open space: voidness or the unconscious in Buddhist terms. This traditional process is an attempt at self integration with mental health. Perhaps the activity of meditation to achieve mental health appears simple, but first the practice is difficult and true meditative enlightenment is rare; and second, the belief system is based on the concept of self integration into a complete universe for general well being. In other words, the act to human health rests upon the acknowledgement of a piecing together process: parts to the whole. Having health is the intuition of reality and identity. It is an aesthetic endeavor. The process and its difficulty depends on the contemplative dwelling on the whole (*dhyāna*) in the spiritual sense of self (*ātma*). It is the knowing we live to whither away (*anicca*). So, human success depends upon a self-knowing, or a human-knowing of the natural conditions and constraints of life. A comprehensive understanding makes a person a candidate for highly cultivated self-observation. A contemplative culture or environment provides the ethos for the appropriate reflection on the spiritualness of physical form (*rupa*) and mental capacity (*nāma*). Together, this binary forms a relationship for human function. The *nāma* capacity is divided into the components of cognitive faculties. The interaction of the mind and the physical world of countless aggregates (*khandhas*) depends on a mental picture (imagination). The grace or aesthetic mood of the person extends from a redefined contemplative mental posture. A satisfying balance is the spirit of health. Only a whole vision is soothing to the Sinhalese. The vision of fragments creates discomfort and eventual illness. Only when the fragments of things (e.g., mental components) are reunited, the person gains a sense of completeness. Among the Sinhalese, meditation is healing in the sense that the self is reintegrated into the mainstream of the living process.

I will present traditional ways of entering different mental states for the intentional healing of the self by personal integration in the institutional devices of *meditation, pilgrimage*, and *ritual performance* where the person acts in the process of cultural parenthesis.

Meditation

Already the Sinhalese aesthetic system has been discussed as a determining factor in each of the life accounts. Here I will present meditation scaled as a universal Sinhalese cultural pattern. The value of meditation is supreme at each level of the belief system. Perhaps, here I should not refer to levels as the Sinhalese people generally utilize meditation as a format for a *persona* or *masks* in the tradition.

In the case of *vipassanā* meditation, the self is the element of introspection. In the act of meditation, time is utilized by sitting long hours in total silence with precise awareness to the personal breathing process— inhale and exhale. The rising and falling of the diaphragm marks the sensation of life. The vital breath is used as a regulatory device to transfer the rational preoccupied mind to a state of internal or universal awareness. The intentional process of focusing on breath is slow and painful, but cumulative to the point of sufficient arrival to the subliminal mind. In the event of mindfulness, the thinking process of the individual is focused into a point of concentration beneath the contextual forms of society (Ven. Rahula 1974:67). Then, the internal stimuli (noninterferring awareness) of the individual takes over the outside sensory adversions (Walsh

1977:151). The result of this kind of aware entry is the direction of emptiness. At first the emptiness is only a relaxed flash (see Lerner 1977). Then it becomes a bright glow seemingly at the center of the body.

Roger Walsh (1977) in his "Initial Meditative Experiences" states *vipassanā* meditation aims at a simple nonjudgemental, noninterferring precise awareness and examination of whatever mental or physical phenomena enter awareness (mindfulness). Meditation, like any deep contemplation, is a device to self awareness. I have found through my meditative experiences in Śrī Lankā the practice of meditation opens the person to another dimension; another state of consciousness. *Vipassanā* or insight meditation is the in-depth self awareness process beyond the normative discursive awareness level in daily life. This means concentration and self examination as a trained scientist observes the subject of study. Meditation is a discipline to discover the newness of the inner life that is universally human.

Meditation is a useful device for entering a different plane of cognitive reality. The illusion is we believe we are held by the active external world. So, people act as social beings. Setting the boundary of human actions is a social process which is bound to waking circumstances.

Among the Sinhalese, meditation is highly regarded. I have spoken of *vipassanā* meditation, but in the more general behavior, the practice is more subtle and ephemeral as its usage in daily life. This is plain self and human awareness. Many laymen are conscious of the value of self reflection and disciplined actions. Human awareness comes from the correct or moral intention of one's activities. That is to say the limitation or the sharing of activities with in the human groups with mindful intentions for a collective moral system creates a more cultivated society.

The headmonk spoke of meditation as a traditional practice in the *sangha*. He even constructed a *kuti* (a meditation shelter) for a monk following and teaching the path of meditation. This strict traditional approach to remain seated in the lotus position of the seated Buddha is regarded as *bhāvanā* (universal meditation in the Sinhalese society). But, the headmonk regarded simply the correct life of mindfulness (*viveka*) to be as important to him as a village monk living in interface with the lay community. This approach was the way he handled routine situations, calmly and thoughtfully for the attention of everybody. The headmonk used his repertoire of experience and gentle disgression in order to make daily decisions. This attitude of *viveka*, or the composed aesthetic life, carried the monk as an effective administrator. His decisions were highly received and accepted by the community because of his training, experience, and philosophical attitude based on the discipline of mindfulness.

The *basnāyaka nilamē* acquired occasional training in *bhāvanā*. He was always a novice or an experimenter in meditation. The *basnāyaka nilamē* preferred to work in the tradition for his family and society at large. His stage of meditation was to rest at home with a grandchild or youngster and smoke or read a newspaper. To him, the daily routine was handled in such a way that business was conducted and forwarded without nervous tension. While filming H. B. Dissanayake as he prepared and proceeded with the Äsala *perahära* festival on his first occasion as "lord," I observed this chief administrator of the shrine became head, participant, and observer at the same time in calm grace and dignity.

The *gurunnānse*, of the three case studies, showed the most extreme practice of "meditation" in the form of his traditional work. The behavior of the exorcism warranted concentration of movement and body action.[3] Every gesture was finely articulated in the dance of exorcism. Health was effected by the precise movements and behavioral structure was predetermined in his crafts, such as mask carving and local dance instruction.

Bhāvanā or meditation is a living value. It is valued as a cultural treasure among the participants of the society and as a concentrated cultural state of consciousness which allows the individual to realize the self and connect as a respected cultural format.

Pilgrimage

The rich
will make temples for Śiva.
What Shall I,
a poor man,
do?

My legs are pillars,
the body the shrine,
the head the cupola
of gold.

---

[3] See the study of Gregory Bateson and Margaret Mead (1942) entitled *Balinese Character: A Photographic Analysis* which clearly illustrates the exacting concentration and procedure of dance and traditional performance trance.

Listen, O lord of the meeting rivers,
things standing fall,
but the moving ever shall stay.

—Kannada Verse
Basavanna (*circa* 820 A.D.)
(Ramanujan 1973:19)

William LaFleur (1979) wrote an article entitled, "Points of Departure: Comments on Religious Pilgrimage in Śrī Lankā and Japan," which examines the concept of Victor Turner's *communitas* in the context of people leaving their daily activities and following a holy path to a spiritual destination: the state of pilgrimage as an attractive alternative to the waking everyday state of awareness. And, again this is a relationship between the individual and the groups engaged in the journey. There are many personal and cultural reasons why people take the pilgrimage, but certainly the most overarching rationale is to commune with others in movement. This is what Victor Turner means by the continuance of "...an entire modality of human social existence..." (*ibid.*:271). The rituals and "holy states" are connected to this very experiential "doing" awareness. I say this because according to Victor Turner, the pilgrimage is outside the usual and "rational" existence as the traveler is on the road to a holy place of miracles. Gananath Obeyesekere (1975:31) points out that pilgrims become part of a new awareness of themselves in a "group solidarity" as in Durkheim's view. In the process of the new vision of this *communitas*, an individual "...strains toward universalism and openness" to the group and the external world (Turner 1974:202). As meditation offers another dimension to the world, the journey to the shrine gives direct access to another state of commitment.

In Śrī Lankā, a pilgrimage entails a journey (*gamana*) for religious adherents from their home village to a shrine at some distance. It is a multi-dimensional occasion where people of every age suffer the hardship of travel and the pleasure of being in a different place, enjoying festivities, the relief of fulfilling a vow or a purpose, and the happiness of returning home to familiar activities. In the progress of the pilgrimage, there is much merry-making among the youths who experience the journey.

The headmonk viewed pilgrimage to be a "youthful" activity at any age. He only joined a pilgrimage when he was invited for religious reasons. Usually a monk participates with laymen on the pilgrimage in order to keep the theme of a religious process. Thus, the headmonk went to the auspicious places in Śrī Lankā; and he joined group journeys to India and Burma. Although the headmonk observed the importance of activity change and religious respect at the sacred shrines, he came to believe later in his life that the inner journey for mental rest (e.g., *viveka*) was the way of an aged monk.

The *basnāyaka nilamē* found the journey, religious or otherwise, was an outlet from the daily administrative tasks. His relations with traditional authority gave him privilege to organize journeys to the various shrines. During World War II, H. B. Dissanayake was able to travel the oceans and foreign lands. While in the military, he visited Jerusalem and the holy sites of pilgrimage. In 1981, H. B. Dissanayake recounted several journeys in Śrī Lankā, and he was preparing to visit those and other historic sites.

As chief of the shrine, the *basnāyaka nilamē* dressed in grand vestments to walk each night of the Āsaḷa *perahāra* festival in a symbolic journey around the shrine or through the town's streets as a ceremonial pilgrimage from the shrine to the *sinhāsanaya* (secular royal seat) and return (Swearer 1982). The people of the *rājakāriya* (tenants of *dēvāle* lands) and the "lord" carried and escorted the image of the deity and related symbols and weapons for the tour. The processional activities included the cracking of whips, drumming and music making, local dancing, a man twirling on a pole, an elderly woman dancing on a suspended tight rope, and decorated elephants marching. The group and onlookers crowded the way in honor of the deity, to gain a blessing, and to be entertained. The social function of work and service for the deity supports and delights the entire community.

The *gurunnānse* joined friends and relations to visit the holy shrines in the Southern Province. The main shrine of Kataragama in Ruhuna is in fairly easy access to the *gurunnānse* and his family. A bus ride would take less than a half day. But, other shrines were also visited in the northern parts of the country. The *gurunnānse* managed a journey to the shrine with pride. On pilgrimage, he would engage in discussions on healing performance (his art and profession) and come upon incidental encounters with associates and other pilgrims on the road in passage. The *gurunnānse* journeyed as the South Indian sage Basavanna who spoke impromtu verse and performed pilgrimage rather than reside in a permanent dwelling. The devotees of this sage were in constant movement visiting the places where the other sages made their camps. Their verses reflected a *protest* to the fixed-place temple builders. As the tradition of shrines became increasingly static in form and function, some people (e.g., devotees of Śiva and local South Indian deities) spoke of a distinction between *building* a temple and *going* as a temple. Pilgrims interpreted the temple as their bodies and became a "living shrine." Performance became more popular than the stone structure; and people undertook the condition of vows to visit the holy camps. While partaking in a geographic journey, people entered in *communitas* as equal beings in the process of personal achievement.

According to my own experiences in South Asia, the pilgrimage is a joy and arduous. But, I developed the skills of doing with less, cooking and eating on the road, interacting in close-proximity with fellow travelers, mastering endurance, and feeling a sense of devotion at the shrine. As I traveled with monks and villagers to the various shrines, I found *communitas* as described by Victor Turner to be a proper formula. In the context of South Asia, other specific dimensions came into play: to have a personal relationship with the group and deity. This is a spiritual body-to-body relationship in the belief system.[4]

Ritual Performance
(Healing and Entertainment)

Altering health is a condition of *karma*, temptation, and impermanence. During the progress of the monastery research, a layman in Hanchāpola gave me an English book to read entitled *Buddhism: My Conception of it*. It was a book written in the late 1930s by R. L. Soni and published later by the Mahā Bodhi Society in Calcutta, India. My impression after reading it was the author had given a very personal account of his encounter, belief, and conversion to Buddhism. According to Buddhist philosophy, the human life is tempted by various pleasures ending in *dukkha* (suffering). Incessant change and illusion (*māyā*) seldom allows the person to achieve a perception of reality:

> Therefore world is Dukkha—naked or veiled it is Dukkha... Life is conditioned by Impermanence: it is suffering—physical and mental: it is void of Reality (Soni 1945:27).

The task of healing in Śrī Lankā is a multi-dimensional process of several specific alternatives. The different healing practices available to the people are first monastic services; second, the system of *āyurveda* medicine, which is "based on a physiological theory of three humors (*tridoṣa*)—wind, bile, and phlegm—which exist in the human body and are responsible for its condition" (Amarasingham 1980:73); third, Western medicine specialized in the treatment of disease through the administration of medication and the practice of surgery; fourth, ecstatic ritual performances of exorcists; and fifth, the use of sorcery or magic for altering health.

Healers among the Sinhalese work according to separate ideosociological theories (see Kapferer 1983). One style, as in exorcism, is

---

[4] See note 1 of chapter *The Kataragama Dēvāle and Basnāyaka Nilamē.*

to face and call off or out pathogenic spirit types. A monk may use a *mantra*, pure water, and a sacred thread. A village physician (*veda mahattayā*) might employ herbal infusions and dietary programs to restore a bodily "equilibrium" in the client. The practitioners deal with a person in an independent way using circumscribed knowledge that does not depend necessarily on other specific areas of knowledge in the culture (Young 1978).

In the monastic tradition, meditation is used as a means of personal reunification in a group. Ritual healing in a village community means the patient is reintroduced to normal society by agents. The monks usually practice meditation (*bhāvanā*) or maintain themselves in a composed attitude (*viveka*) on a daily basis.

In terms of healing a person inflicted with illness, the monks will perform an active *pirit* ceremony to purify an individual by forcing "evil" from the body. This event occurs when there is a *person, space,* or *new building* in need of purification (R. Obeyesekere 1990:118-124). Monks will collectively perform the ritual of purification.

The ceremony is essentially held by monks who chant the words of the Buddha in the original Pāli language to expel inhabiting evil spirits. Sometimes the monks are seated in an elaborate *pirit maṇḍapa* for the occasion. The chanting proceeds for an hour, or from sunset to sunrise; and sometimes for several nights. While reciting verses from memory, the monks grasp and hold a sacred thread (*nūla*) that is tied to a blessed new clay pot of water (usually as the spatial center of the ritual) and extends away to the seated participants and laity. The ceremony concludes with the cutting and tying of the long thread to the wrists of the lay persons present. Sanctified water is sprinkled from the pot (*pūrṇa kumbha*) on the participating laity by a monk.

In the motion picture about the headmonk, a *pirit* ritual is shown in a rural domestic home. The patient is a cultivator who has a fever. The family of the man goes to the headmonk of the monastery to ask for religious assistance. The headmonk decides on a *pirit* ceremony to spiritually assist the villager and he calls on villagers to participate in the man's cultivation work.

The film sequence of the *pirit* ceremony showed three monks chanting near the patient. A village medical practitioner tied the thread to the *pūrṇa kumbha* and unrolled the thread off a spool to the monks and patient. The monks (agents) chanted while seated on white honorific cloth. They kept their faces partially veiled behind palm leaf fans. Close family members stayed in adjoining rooms. When the ceremony was complete, the headmonk broke and tied a piece of thread on the patient's wrist.

The ritual was very codified and strict in the formal sense. But as a ceremonial occasion, people not directly involved in the ritual proceedings interact at the fringe—as they are entertained by it (see Goffman 1982, Kapferer 1975). The fringe people depend on the spectacle dimensions of the ceremony. A *pirit* ceremony usually attracts a sober crowd, but nevertheless, some people join to enjoy the qualities of ritual "bracketing" of the daily activities.

Some people of religious mindedness have developed themselves into a conscious mental state of devoted tranquility. For them, the ceremony is a slight extension of their daily practice of sitting long hours and moving among people in a disciplined way.

In terms of healing, the social solidarity and humanity displayed in the ritual process connects the people together with the patient in a defined state of illness. The ceremony is beneficial for the belief system and the participating community. In the commonness of collectivity, people are soothed; and each person receives a piece of the sanctified thread.

In the *basnāyaka nilame's* realm, the greatest healing act is held in the Kataragama Dēvāle compound where people crowd the grounds for enjoyment and ritual performance. It is a functional shrine where people unfold themselves amidst an array of playful and spiritually directed pilgrims. Healing is the theme for the multiplicity of people attending the shrine.

The Äsala festival takes place during the month following the Vesak full moon marking the Buddha's birthday, enlightenment, and passing away. It recognizes the first sermon preached by the Buddha: Dhammacakkappavattana Sutta.

In an article in the *Weekend*, Sunday, July 13, 1980 entitled "Mystery of Kataragama's Divine Force," the writer Dionysius de Silva announced:

> The Esala [Äsala] festival at Kataragama commenced yesterday (Saturday). Large crowds of pilgrims are drawn to this sylvan shrine during the festive period, seeking the aid of a divine being to overcome their miseries, ailments and worries. To whom do these thousands of pilgrims perform various acts of devotion.

Continued:

> Holding a husked coconut right above the head in both hands and rolling in the Dēvāle premises is a common sight. Sticking of well-pointed leaf-like shapes called 'vel' in silver to the skin of the chest and back and arms, piercing the cheeks with pointed silver spikes and fixing hooks to the skin to which are tied either a rope tethered to a cart with the

God's image; walking on nailed sandals with the pointed end touching the soles of the feet, suspending one's body on a scaffold on hooks embedded into the skin; carrying pots of burning camphor on the head or palms; gazing at the sun with widely opened eyes are various forms of poojas [pujas] in fulfillment of vows and fire-walking ceremony.

The performance of healing takes on the relationship of etiquette, tact, timing, and sensitivity. A healing-practitioner takes the time to know and interact with the patient and family in question "since patient and public share the same definition of Reality, which we call culture, cognitive disorientation is warded off" (Obeyesekere 1981:104):

> Yet the *effective* performance of the shaman role requires certain psychological propensities (the capacity to be possessed by a deity [i.e., spirit]) that can best be realized by a prior, psychologically isomorphic illness—that is, a possession experience that is subsequently tamed and brought under both ego and cultural control (*ibid.*:42).

> Without this kind of deep motivation, shamanism may well become a formal priestly religion, without much dynamism (*ibid.*).

Healing in the process of exorcism is an expression of the patient coping with illness or disease and the practice of the exorcist is to label the specifics (see Tambiah 1970:327–336). First the exorcist must decide what is the particular manifestation of the illness. The exorcist usually diagnoses illness which is human "*experiences* of disvalued changes of being and in social function" (Eisenberg 1977:11). In contrast, disease has the distinction of referring to a special biomedical concept as "disorders in the chemistries and physiologies of the individual" (Fabrega 1978:14). For disease, the Sinhalese generally seek attention from a Western educated professional of medicine. Because disease is usually organic and clinically treated in a sanitary room without the support of affective friends and close relations, sometimes the procedure of the physician is limited to the biological ailment. But, the Sinhalese prefer to have options and a range of alternative procedures functioning in the practice of the health system.

People going to the *dēvāle* will ask a *kapurāla* for a good word or blessing from the deity, a purification ritual from Buddhist monks—or the act of an exorcist as alternatives to treatment from a hospital physician educated in the Western theory of health care. Illness is perceived when the individual is in an apparent state of anxiety.[5] A health system expert is sought after who should be able to categorize the anomie: according to

---

[5] Illness is a range of anxieties which disorients the individual as with the case of hypertension (Bar-Lev 1982) when psychologically coping with problems.

Sinhalese theory—it is a general disarray of the human system. The causes of illness are usually evil and in self disarray. So, the health practitioner must classify and match symptoms with the evil or harmful forces. The spirit/illness labeling process sorts an apparently unfamiliar disorder into something classifiable. Thus the practitioner's client becomes reinstated by the process reducing ambiguity and maintaining the social presence of the person.

The role of the *gurunnānse* is to enforce the belief system's triad by revealing the discipline and moral ways of the Buddha, the benevolence and power of the deities, and the tricks and guise of the evil spirits. It is believed that when the Buddha mythically landed in Śrī Lankā, he delivered a sermon to the evil spirits to appease them. The evil spirits were only acting out their *kamma*. So, eventually the Buddha impressed the deities to the way of "right action," and he entrusted deities to stabilize the evil spirit situation if they created chaos. It is the exorcist who will go through the ritual of treatment with the aid of deities to pacify the evil spirits.

The *gurunnānse* of my study had a vast knowledge of the spells and magical formulas from his apprenticeship days. Also equally important, he expressed a range of human understanding qualities. By working intimately with people inflicted with illness, the *gurunnānse* displayed a repertoire of professional empathy: a disciplined knowing of another person's experience without necessarily encountering that experience personally. This is a quality that other practitioners (i.e., monks, *vederālas, kapurālas*) find more difficult to achieve because of their formalized dealings with people.

A *gurunnānse* or *yakadurā* must be distinguished from fortunetellers who deal with planetary designs and horoscopes, *kapurālas* who are the priests of deity shrines, and *vederālas* who administer traditional Sinhalese medicine. The exorcist constructs a magic and temporary shrine to attract evil. It is temporary because the people want the evil spirits to only pass-by and look at the situation and then leave. In contrast *dēvāle* priests (*kapurālas*) have a permanent and established shrine where they transact holy Buddhist/deity business at specific hours on a daily basis. The exorcist's temporary shrine is elaborate to the state of representing a woven palace (*vīdiya*) of bamboo, banana-tree trunks, palm leaves, and decorated with flowers to compose geometric designs. In the process of making the ill-self to the well-self, the exorcist defines the evil or benevolent spirit inhabiting the patient. The labeling process is very precise as the exorcist is able to enter the patients reality of suffering.

The exorcist does not reprimand or censor the evil spirits but he actively enjoins them to share in a feast and observe their own unsightly manifestations portrayed by the exorcist and his troupe. With crafted masks and costumes, the healers perform in front of the patient in a court bounded by their temporary shrine, posts and baskets of food offerings, and the crowd. The performance is a display of human offering to the evil spirits so that they will be satisfied and leave the premises.

The philosophy of tolerance, the love of diversity and action, and the concept that all things change provides for the atmosphere of the dynamic qualities. Each ritual performance whether it be in a tranquil temple or in the dust of a village courtyard is a place where the people are "entertained." In terms of the exorcist's ritual, the performer is ecstatic to the fine point of reaching the patient. The performance is precise yet mixed (*accāru*) with various popular characterizations: "movie stars and characters often (infamous) encountered in everyday life" (Kapferer 1977:91, and 1983).

The public enjoys ritual performance. A patient suffers and recovers (or not) in the progressive arena of popular and collective purification as an application to a higher sense of authority. The specialists who make it happen are the active agents. Collective support and comfort comes form the close family and society at large.

The process is a system of illness definition and a social display of identification and recovery. Entertainment is a ritual manifestation which holds patient/public attention to the event of healing in the arena of communicative symbols which culturally speak effectively. The rejoining process is a celebration.

Conclusion

Epilogue

I am one with them yet not one of them.

—Gananath Obeyesekere 1981:11

The value of ethnographic research is a kind of initiation into understanding another belief system as an inter-personal agreement of the reciprocal procedures in terms of the community which was studied. In terms of myself, the rationale behind doing ethnography is to create a portrait or cultural document for the participant individuals or community. This concept stems from a moral determination to share with the participants the material from the research. Thus, the research remains intelligible for the participant community. In terms of my performance, the "ethnographic encounter" is a life commitment. The model/research design, ethnographic research, presentation of ethnography/stage to public, and feedback/review circle is an upward cycle to new research perspectives. Yet the entire endeavor remains provisional as anthropologists have discovered.

> Research in the social sciences is like the search for a new "mythic charter" for humanity—the charter under which we currently live having become jumbled and contested—but no matter what facts we discover in our genes or in history, the image of human nature that we construct from them will not surpass the charter stage, will never be totally determining, because it will be incomplete and because, to appear true, it will require human faith and energy (Riesman 1977:38).

My perspective is that ethnographic research and the presentation of the resulting ethnography should be accurate and specific, yet with alternatives for variation on uses. Of course, ethnography should match its goals in terms of the orientation and direction of the research design.

> The advancement of research procedure in social science as elsewhere depends on making explicit what researchers actually do ...(Barton and Lazarsfeld 1955:321, cited by Honigmann 1976:243).

I have been interested in ethnography as a multi-dimensional integrated process mindful of the integrity of each process and unit in the task. The personal approach in research is very appealing to me, but I also feel statistical research—with a more sociological bearing as Emile Durkheim's famous case study on suicide—is also a very humanistic method for the ordering of things. A diverse methodological approach with regard for separate items is the key. Mogoroh Maruyama (1974) in his article "Symbiotization of

151

Cultural Heterogeneity: Scientific, Epistemological, and Esthetic Bases,"
recalls that in his prison research it was useful to work *for* and *with* the in-
mates just as much as for the sponsors of the research. Maruyama's point is
the so-called "Eastern" or "indigenous" paradigm (logic of heterogeneity):
that is to say, there is fundamental harmony in dissimilar elements or persons. Western science is interested in mainstreaming in a single path of one
universal objective truth because Western history proves there is psychological security in homogeneous logic (Halsey 1963). The one authority idea
stems from a Western "contemporary" concept of the Judeo-Christian philosophy using the deity system as a standardization metaphor. When one
figure or authority has a monopoly on the "correct" way of doing things,
then polarization to mixed patterns sets in. Strength in research policy
depends on sharing in terms of interdependent mutualism. Ninian Smart
(1973:37) presents three points in belief systems research methodology:

(1) a matter of human symbiosis,

(2) synchronic description,

(3) multi-dimensional structure in terms of aspects of evidence i.e., texts,
    psychology, history, personality.

> The fact is that we [researchers] are on the same level with what we
> study, when we study humans behaving religiously, and it is this that
> is particularly responsible for the reflexive effect of the study of religion
> upon religion.

Symbiotic research sharing is an ideal. Certainly there must be a direction and purpose. Many research compromises are forced rather than
embraced with comfort. My counterparts or associates among the Sinhalese take leave from their usual occupations, go in opposite directions,
and spend money to assist in anthropological research. But, they assisted
on the research tasks because of friendship and cultural interest. Perhaps
genuine synthesis of support would not have developed just for the sake
of the research. My ideal of a mutualization process in research is only a
working model as in Paul Riesman's "charter." But even in its immediate
circumstances, the research is useful. Since my role began with the collection of life accounts, apart from this present research, I have found I
have entered the realm not only of another culture, but of another person
in time. My research journeys to Śrī Lankā and other areas of South and
Southeast Asia have given me a breadth of knowledge concerning personal
traits and behaviors in so many ways of doing things. The genuineness of
observing culture and ordering in my mind what I *see* and *experience* is my
reward. This research comes from my training as a participant-observer in
anthropology. That is to say, the trained ethnographer allows spontaneous
and traditional meanings to emerge from the process of the personal and

cultural relationships. Once the sharing relationship has been chartered with specific intentions, the participants can attend to their dialogue. Observation of the participants and the self is the anthropological *tool* for the experiential task of entering into a dialogue to *understand* and *record* the meanings the person gives to social phenomena. The ethnographer has the chance to observe the participants in the richness of cultural context.

The ethnographer must "tune-in" as in the "mutual tuning-in relationship" stated by Alfred Schutz (1967:108) to the relationship with an *intentional* "gaze perception" in order to distinguish the shades of life flowing in change. With sufficient attention to the dialogue, the related image/impressions of the participant can be focused upon to make coherent arrangements for a life account. The ethnographer attends to the relationship design as "the speaker always chooses his words with the listener's interpretation in mind" (*ibid.*:128). As the participant regards the researcher the person's mental selection of experiences and values operate in anticipation of the listener's behavior (e.g., response). Anticipation—that reflexive looking forward—gives the orientation to the related experiences in the dialogue: as every past action is pictured in the present (*ibid.*:59). In the dialogue, the ethnographer records those experiences related by the participant as presented in terms of memory and *the here and now* relationship.

The ethnographer copes with the vagueness of the person's memory conditioned by emotion, working-order, and age. The vagueness remains with the person. Skilled psychoanalysis reveals the hidden, so-called forgotten, experiences. The most private dreams will not readily emerge to be shared. Individuals in the dream state are in the "self telling" and social integration process. The dream consciousness acts as an aesthetic index to reality very much as in the sense of cultural mythological experience. The dream as a mythic state is useful for the person and for the analyst or ethnographer in their understanding of "deep" motivation.

In ethnography, dreams are just being touched upon (Bourguignon 1972).[1]

> Yet, while the subjects of dreams and dreaming are touched upon in ethnographies in general, and particularly in those focusing on certain subject matters such as religion or personality structure, dreams and dreaming have only rarely been the principle targets of major ethnographic or comparative studies (*ibid.*:405–406).

---

[1] For works concerning *dreams* in "ethnographic" context see Seligmann 1923, Firth 1934, Eggan 1949, Devereux 1951, Eliade 1960, D'Andrade 1961, and Kuper 1979, (Eggan and D'Andrade review the literature).

Rodney Needham, in his *Primordial Characters* (1978:64) states that concerning dreams:

> ...the greater part of the materials out of which dreams are composed is probably cultural; but some components are so practically universal, as are the operations to which they are subjected, that they cannot be ascribed to the differentiating influences of culture.

The ethnographer allows the spontaneous meanings to emerge from the dialogue process of the relationship. In the ethnographer's orientation, the experiences of the person must be actualized and pictured at the moment of projection. As a person relates experience to another person or thing without natural boundaries, the ethnographer must start to organize the life process into frames. Only when the ethnographer reflects into the individual or intentionally contemplates on the dialogue in the *present* can the detail of the experience be arranged. In the presentation, the ethnography should flow with the participants own pattern.[2]

The life account composition is a matter of mental and aesthetic organization. The recognition of human patterns can result from the contemplation or introspection of the composition of oneself. Regardless of the point of reflection, the ethnographer has the *keys* of experience and awareness in order to cultivate the patterns out of the spectrum of human experiences and objects.

> The methodologies of all true sciences are rational, involving, as they do, the use of formal logic and interpretive schemes. All true sciences demand the maximum of clarity and distinctness for all their propositions... Science remains a matter of thought even when its subject matter is life (Schutz 1967:240).

The ethnographer "grasps" those experiences which are expressed by another individual and arranges the impressions into a rational and aesthetic description. The related experience clusters and flashes of insight which are shared in the cultural space (context) become the data for operational use. The ethnographer utilizes intuition, imagination, and skill to recognize patterns and present them in a coherent way. The specific idiom depends on the gathering process.

The dilemma of the life account is the one which has shaded social studies because the question of the artist and the scientist comes into play.

---

[2] See Dan Rose's article (1982) "Occasions and Forms of the Anthropological Experience" concerning experience and aesthetic display in presenting ethnography; and for validity in terms of "ethnographic novel" writings see L. L. Langness and Gelya Frank 1978; and, see James Clifford and George E. Marcus (1986).

If we "observe" the inside of a person or the nature of an object by contemplative means, then how is the experience recorded for the anthropologists at large to comprehend? There must be a way to communicate the experience. This is where the artist emerges in the use of communication tools to expose an ethnographic "mind's eye" to track any human event:

Music is the best cultural medium to portray the essential energy of a human in a natural world. This is because music is a non-specific and temporal process as it is not bound to space—music is like time itself.

Painting and any other static or semi-mobile art like photography or sculpture is a valid form to present a life symbol; but not a dynamic life account. Unlike music which flows, a painting is static and spatial. This means that the content represented as an image is complete as it stands. What comes from the image in the form of information depends on the patience or impatience of the viewer (e.g., the observer seated in contemplation in front of a painting, or the observer just walking by the painting to see it at a glance).

Motion picture is the visual art which is fluid as music and remains framed on the screen as a static painting. It is the art which most *represents* live action, yet it is only various shaded light tones shining on a screen, with the potential or act of motion.

Surely the presentation is ethnography itself. The display of individuals or cultural dimensions impart meaning to match or stimulate awareness and sensitivity.

The ethnographic challenge is as large as the ethnographer. For that charter, the ethnographer must remain flexible yet formalized to the next step. The selection and organization process of material gives discrete units and labels for data distinction. The ethnographer organizes the living data into written and/or visual structure with interconnecting and continuous frames. If successful, the aesthetic quality of the presented ethnographic interpretation and resulting meaning will emerge.

For this present research of the three individuals, the methodological philosophy and procedure as presented in the Introduction and Perspectives remained as a guide. I worked interdependently for the outcome with participants and colleagues. What I have written should be read in the context of Southern Asia, but the methodological approach to research in terms of personal interaction was written to be standard (see Rittenberg 1977).

As I lived the process of *growing old together* with a Sinhalese participant in order to record another person's way of life, I will present a selection of thoughts on research expressing cultural values:

(1) The ethnographer can not act with impunity.

(2) Explanation should always be given to participants.

(3) The ethnographic plan should be reviewed and discussed with participants in order to receive mutual feedback.

(4) Objectivity is a conviction like faith bound in one's own experience of thought or feeling.

(5) The presented ethnography should be intrinsically interesting, that is to say, an aesthetic quality must be a total composition: sense of balance, environmental orientation, and display to the audience in mind.

(6) Sacred areas are defined by faith, not by material structures alone.

(7) The life history or ethnography as organized remembered experiences should be assembled in a way participants can accept.

(8) The ethnographer should keep in mind the long range effects of the ethnography in terms of the participants, their cultural future, and the anthropological literature.

For me the philosophical dimensions remain richly profound as in the case of most ethnographers. The religious men taught me important ways of living without specifically instructing me. I was impressed by their discipline and insight. In this book, I have presented the participants as they have displayed themselves to me. This method created ideal images. But, as Akemi Kikumura (1981) has shown in the life writing from her mother's account, a person's own stories maintain the essential unity of the being. The individual pattern of continuity is inherent; and the philosophy of a life will resound true or false, clouded or focused. Each life account is extremely concise compared to the actual lived life. How brief is it? How honest? My intention has been to record lives and learn. The image of those men will always be with me. From the Sinhalese research, I have entered a constant review on life.

I have felt my resesarch in rural areas has encouraged me to further concentrate on the relevance of cultures woven in our daily life and how values are understood (Frelich 1989). This research was a rich experiential endeavor in which I entered a new way of life in the context of Mr. A. L. Perera's family for a perspective as well as sense of belonging in Sinhalese society. The methods in anthropology are important for the results and bearing a consciousness (Obeyesekere 1981). These *ways and means* should reflect the attitude of a people; based on the environment (Kabilsingh 1988, Kwai and Lun 1988, Batchelor and Brown 1992), value of landscape design

(Duncan 1990), economic interests (Gunawardana 1979), and the heritage of celebration in a place where struggling for basic stabilized identity is the order of the day. Where an old state turns on the contemporary stage, the measure of the institutions depends on the dynamics of individuals who work on *life* questions. The dynamics of the belief system is the test in religious pluralism (Chappell 1990). In terms of the ceremonial state, colonial influence has lost much force and yet the newer values are yet to become a new force (Manning 1983:11).

*   *   *

This research began in 1973, and continued over the years. I started with an interest in the *rājakāriya* (land tenure system) and later looked at the complete belief system. As anthropological tools gave power to this study, I persisted in utilizing multi-dimensional media such as the camera, life history, and the theoretical construct required to get a holistic bearing on the Buddhist belief system. After the passing of time, I observed the Sinhalese in their process of development and their despair; but, as I continued to research in Śrī Lankā, I have been convinced of a positive strength which has sustained the culture since the pre-colonial era. In my research, I have tried to understand this strength of cultural persistence. The original issues such as *rājakāriya* continue and the views given and guided by the people to me, have provided the contextual understanding of this society.

Serapinda, wood carving, Embekke Dēvāle
(Wijesekera 1984, *pl.* 144)

References

Selected Abbreviations

AA	*American Anthropologist*
BSOAS	*Bulletin of School of Oriental and African Studies*
JAS	*Journal of Asian Studies*
ISHI	*Institute for the Study of Human Issues, Inc.*
RAIN	*Royal Anthropological Institute News*
SAVICOM	Society for the Anthropology of Visual Communication
UC	University of California

Abel, Theodore 1948 "The Operation Called *Verstehen*," *American Journal of Sociology*, 54(3):211–218.

Allport, Gordon W. 1950 *The Individual and His Religion*. NY: Macmillan.

Amarasingham, L. R. 1980 "Movement Among Healers in Śrī Lankā: A Case Study of a Sinhalese Patient," *Culture, Medicine and Psychiatry*, 4(1):71–89.

Ames, Michael 1961 "A Structural Analysis of Sinhalese Religion," *Proceedings of the Seminar on Indian Religions*, UC Berkeley, August.

———. 1963 "Ideological and Social Change in Ceylon," *Human Organization*, 22(1):45–53.

———. 1966 "Ritual Presentations and the Structure of the Sinhalese Pantheon," *Studies in Theravāda Buddhism*. M. Nash, ed., Cultural Report Series, 13 (Yale University Southeast Asia Studies) pp. 27–50.

———. 1969 "The Impact of Western Education on Religion and Society in Ceylon," *Śrī Lankārāmaya Vesak Annual 1969*, pp. 67–75.

Amore, Roy C. and Larry D. Shinn 1981 *Lustful Maidens and Ascetic Kings: Buddhist and Hindu Stories of Life*. NY: Oxford University Press.

Anesaki, Masaharu 1915 *Buddhist Art in its relation to Buddhist Ideal, with Special Reference to Buddhism in Japan*. Boston: Houghton Miffin Co.

Appadurai, Arjun 1981 "The Past as a Scarce Resource," *Man*, 16(2):201–219.

Arieti, Silvano 1980 "Cognition in Psychoanalysis," *Journal of the American Academy of Psychoanalysis*, 8(1):3–23.

Arnheim, Rudolf 1957 *Film as Art*. Berkeley: UC Press.

——. 1974 *Art and Visual Perception: A Psychology of the Creative Eye*. Berkeley: UC Press.

Arnold, Sir Edwin 1879 *The Light of Asia*. London: Trubner.

Balikei, Asen 1992 Anthropologists and Ethnographic Filmmaking," *Anthropological Filmmaking: Anthropological Perspectives on the Production of Film and Video for General Public Audiences*, Jack R. Rollwagen, ed., Chur: Harwood Academic Publishers (original 1988) pp. 31–45.

Bandara, H. H. 1972 *Cultural Policy in Śrī Lankā*. Paris: UNESCO.

Bandaranayake, Senake 1974 *Sinhalese Monastic Architecture: The Vihāras of Anurādhapura*. Leiden: E. J. Brill.

——. 1978 Personal communication.

Bandaranayake, Senake and Gamini Jayasinghe 1986 *The Rock and Wall Paintings of Śrī Lankā*. Colombo: Lake House Bookshop.

Banks, John and Judy Banks 1986 *A Selection of the Animals of Śrī Lankā*. Colombo: Lake House Investments Ltd.

Bar-Lev, Sanford S. 1982 "Handling Stress for Hypertension Control," *HBPC News* (High Blood Pressure Council of Los Angeles), Fall.

Barnes, J. A. 1971 *Three Styles in the Study of Kinship*. London: Tavistock.

Barnes, S. B. 1969 "Paradigms—Scientific and Social," *Man* 4(1):94–102.

Barnouw, Victor 1963 *Culture and Personality*. Homewood, IL.: Dorsey Press.

Barton, Allen H. and Paul F. Lazarsfeld 1955 "Some Functions of Qualitative analysis in Social Research," *Sociologica: Aufsatze, Max Horkheimer Zum Sechzigsten Geburtstag Gewidmet*. Stuttgart: Europaishe Verlagsanstalt.

Basham, A. L. 1959 *The Wonder that was India: A Survey of the History and Culture of the Indian Sub-continent before the Coming of the Muslims*. NY: Grove Press (original 1954).

Batchelor, Martine and Kerry Brown 1992 *Buddhism and Ecology.* London: Cassell Publishers Ltd.

Bateson, Gregory 1958 *Naven: A Survey of the Problems Suggested by a Composite Picture of the Culture of a New Guinea Tribe Drawn from Three Points of View.* Stanford, CA: Stanford University Press.

———. 1979 *Mind and Nature: A Necessary Unity.* NY: E.P. Dutton.

Bateson, Gregory and Margaret Mead 1942 *Balinese Character: A Photographic Analysis.* NY: The Academy of Sciences.

Bechert, Heinz and Richard Gombrich, eds. 1984 *The World of Buddhism: Buddhist Monks and Nuns in Society and Culture.* NY: Facts on File.

Becker, A. L. and Aram A. Yengoyan, eds. 1979 *The Imagination of Reality: Essays in Southeast Asian Coherence Systems.* Norwood, NJ: ABLEX Publishing Corp.

Beidelman, Thomas O. 1974 *W. Robertson Smith and the Sociological Study of Religion.* Chicago: University of Chicago Press.

Bellah, R. N. n.d. *Some Suggestions for the Systematic Study of Religion,* ms. Harvard University.

Bellman, Beryl L. and Bennetta Jules-Rosette 1977 *A Paradigm for Looking.* Norwood, NJ: ABLEX Publishing Corp.

Benson, Stella 1929 "Preface: Written in a Bad Temper," *Worlds Within Worlds.* NY: Harper and Brothers Publishers.

Beny, Roloff 1970 *Island Ceylon.* Text by John Lindsay Opie. London: Thames and Hudson.

Berger, Peter and Thomas Luckmann 1967 *The Social Construction of Reality.* London: Allen Lane.

Bernard, Jessie 1949 "The Art of Science: A Reply to Redfield," *The American Journal of Sociology,* 55(1):1–9.

Bettelheim, Bruno 1976 *The Uses of Enchantment.* NY: Knopf.

Bismillah Khan 1967 A motion picture portrait of the "prince of the shenai." Indiana University distribution.

Blundell, David 1979 *The Life History of Ven. Hanchāpola Gnānavansa Thero, A Buddhist Headmonk in Śrī Lankā,* motion picture Sinhala, 1980 English, U-matic video 1984, UCLA, distribution by author.

———. 1980 *The Life of a Basnāyaka Nilamē, and the Badulla Kataragama Dēvāle Perahāra,* motion picture, 40 mins., unpublished.

——. 1981 *The Life and Practice of a Gurunnānse in Southern Śrī Lankā*, motion picture, 20 mins., unpublished.

——. 1991 "Visual Anthropology and Cultural Preservation and Revitalization: Life Visual Account as Community Heritage Document Ven. H. Gnānavansa Thero, Buddhist Monk (1902–1979)," *Visual Anthropology*, 4(1):43–52.

Bourguignon, Erika 1972 "Dreams and Altered States of Consciousness in Anthropological Research," *Psychological Anthropology: Approaches to Culture and Personality*. Francis L. K. Hsu, ed., Cambridge, MA: Schenkman Publishing Company, Inc., pp. 403–434.

——. 1973 "Introduction: A Framework for the Comparative Study of Altered States of Consciousness," *Religion: Altered States of Consciousness, and Social Change*, in her ed. Columbus: Ohio State University Press.

Brand, Stuart 1977 "Margaret Mead and Gregory Bateson on the Use of the Camera in Anthropology," *Studies in Visual Communication*, Sol Worth, ed., 4(2):78–80.

Brant, Charles S., ed. 1969 *Jim White Wolf: The Life of a Kiowa Apache Indian*. NY: Dover Publications, Inc.

Brohm, J. 1963 "Buddhism and Animism in a Burmese Village," *JAS*, 12(2):155–167.

Bronowski, Jacob 1962 *The Common Sense of Science*. NY: Vintage Books.

Brough, John 1959 "The Tripartite Ideology of the Indo-Europeans: An Experiment in Method," *BSOAS*, 22:68–86.

Bruner, Edward M. 1964 "The Psychological Approach in Anthropology," *Horizons of Anthropology*, Sol Tax, ed., Chicago: Aldine Publishing Co., pp. 71–80.

Bruner, Jerome S. 1973 "Beyond the Information Given: Studies in the Psychology of Knowing," J. M. Anglin, ed., NY: Norton.

Byrom, Thomas 1976 *The Dhammapada: The Sayings of the Buddha, a new rendering*. NY: Knopf.

Chalfen, Richard 1983 "The Family Album as an Interpretation of Culture: A Japanese American Case Study," *Japanese American Family Albums: A Los Angeles Family*. Japanese American Cultural and Community Center, Los Angeles, CA; featuring the Motoji Imon family, the George Kambara family, the Sokichi Kataoka family, the Ichihara/Kubo family, the Maruyama family, the Juichi Nawa family, and the George Nagano family. February 20th–May 20th, lecture given March 6th.

Carrithers, Michael B. 1983 *The Forest Monks of Śrī Lankā: An Anthropological and Historical Study.* Delhi: Oxford University Press.

——. 1984 "The will be Lords upon the Island: Buddhism in Śrī Lankā," *The World of Buddhism: Buddhist Monks and Nuns in Society and Culture.* Heinz Bechert and Richard Gombrich, eds., NY: Facts on File, pp. 133–146.

Chappell, David W. 1990 "Buddhist Responses to Religious Pluralism: What Are the Ethical Issues?" presented at the *Chung-hwa International Conference on Buddhism*, National Central Library, Taipei.

Chiozzi, Paolo 1989 "Reflections on Ethnographic Film with a General Bibliography," trans. by Denise Dresner, *Visual Anthropology*, 2(1):1–84.

Clifford, James and George E. Marcus, eds. 1986 *Writing Culture: The Poetics and Politics of Ethnography.* A School of American Research Advanced Seminar. Berkeley: UC Press.

Cole, Michael and Sylvia Scribner 1974 *Culture and Thought: A Psychological Introduction.* NY: John Wiley & Sons, Inc.

Collier Jr., John and Aníbal Buitrón 1949 *The Awakening Valley.* Chicago: University of Chicago Press.

Collier Jr., John and Malcolm Collier 1986 *Visual Anthropology: Photography as a Research Method.* Albuquerque: University of New Mexico Press (original by John Collier Jr., 1967, NY: Holt, Rinehart and Winston series).

Collins, Steven 1990 *Selfless Persons: Imagery and Thought in Theravāda Buddhism.* NY: Cambridge University Press (original 1982).

Cone, Margaret and Richard F. Gombrich 1977 *The Perfect Generosity of Prince Vessantara: A Buddhist Epic.* Oxford: Oxford University Press.

Conze, E. 1959 *Buddhism, Its Essence and Development.* NY: Harper.

Coomaraswamy, Ananda K. 1922 "Introduction," *Dancing and the Drama East and West*, by Stella Block, NY: Orientalia, pp. i–iii.

——. 1942 *Spiritual Authority and Temporal Power in the Indian Theory of Government.* New Haven, CT: American Oriental Society.

——. 1947 *Am I My Brother's Keeper?* NY: The John Day Company.

——. 1956 *Mediaeval Sinhalese Art.* NY: Pantheon (original 1908, Broad Campden: Essex House Press).

——. 1971 *The Dance of Shiva.* New Delhi: Sagar Publications.

Cooper, David 1974 *The Grammar of Living.* NY: Pantheon Books.

Crane, Julia G. and Michael V. Angrosino 1992 *Field Projects in Anthropology: A Student Handbook.* Prospect Heights, IL: Waveland Press, Inc. (original 1984) see pp. 75–87, 150–178.

Crapanzano, Vincent 1972 *The Fifth World of Forster Bennett: Portrait of a Navaho.* NY: Viking Press.

——. 1977a "The Life History in Anthropological Field Work," *Anthropology and Humanism Quarterly,* 2(2–3):3–7.

——. 1977b "The Writing of Ethnography," *Dialectical Anthropology,* 2:69–73.

——. 1980 *Tuhami: Portrait of a Moroccan.* Chicago: University of Chicago Press.

——. 1984 "Life-Histories," *AA,* 86:953-960.

Crawford, Peter I. and Jan K. Simonsen 1992 *Ethnographic Film, Aesthetics and Narrative Tradition — Proceedings from NAFA II.* Højbjerg, Denmark: Intervention Press.

Dahlberg, Edward 1941 *Do These Bones Live?* NY: Harcourt, Brace and Co.

D'Andrade, Roy G. 1961 "Anthropological Studies of Dreams," *Psychological Anthropology: Approaches to Culture and Personality.* Francis L. K. Hsu, ed., Homewood, IL.: The Dorsey Press, Inc., pp. 296-332.

de Brigard, Emilie 1975 "The History of Ethnographic Film," *Toward a Science of Man: Essays in the History of Anthropology.* Timothy H. Thoresen, ed., The Hague: Mouton Publications, pp. 33–63.

de Certeau, M. 1984 *The Practice of Everyday Life.* Berkeley: UC Press.

de Heusch, Luc 1962 *The Cinema and the Social Sciences: A Survey of Ethnographic and Sociological Films.* Paris: UNESCO Reports and Papers in the Social Sciences, 16.

Denzin, Norman 1989 *Interpretive Biography.* Beverly Hills, CA: Sage Press.

de Silva, Deemathie W. 1983 "Spirit Possession: A Case Study from Śrī Lankā," presented at the *Annual Meeting of the Popular Culture Association.,* April 24th.

de Silva, Dionysius 1980 "Mystery of Kataragama's Divine Force," Colombo, *Weekend*. Sunday, July 13th.

de Silva, K. M. 1981 *A History of Śrī Lankā*. Berkeley: UC Press.

de Silva, Lynn 1980 *Buddhism: Beliefs and Practices in Śrī Lankā*. Colombo. Śrī Lankā: Wesley Press (original 1974).

Devereux, George 1951 *Reality and Dream: Psychotherapy of a Plains Indian*. NY: International University.

———. 1967 *From Anxiety to Method in the Behavior Sciences*. The Hauge: Mouton.

———. 1976 *Dreams in Greek Tragedy: An Ethno-Psycho-Analytical Study*. Berkeley: UC Press.

———. 1977 "Society's Stake in Art," *Anthropology Full Circle*. Ino Rossi, John Buettner-Janusch, Dorian Coppenhaver, eds., NY: Praeger Publishers, pp. 406–410.

de Waal Malefijt, Annemarie 1968 *Religion and Culture: An Introduction to Anthropology of Religion*. NY: Macmillan.

de Zoete, Beryl 1957 *Dance and Magic Drama in Ceylon*. London: Faber and Faber Ltd.

Dhammacakkappavattana Suttaṃ. 1879-1883 *Vinaya Piṭakam, (Mahā-vagga)*, vol. 1 of 5 vols., p. 7. Edited by Hermann Oldenberg. London: Williams and Norgate.

Dissanayake, Wimal and Steven Bradbury, eds. 1989 *Literary History, Narrative, and Culture*. Honolulu: University of Hawaii Press.

Dolmatoff, G. Reichel 1975 *The Shaman and the Jaguar*. Philadephia: Temple University Press.

Douglas, Mary 1970 *Natural Symbols: Explorations in Cosmology*. NY: Random House.

du Boulay, J. and Willam R. 1984 "Collecting Life Histories," *ASA Research Methods in Social Anthropology*. London: Academic Press.

Dufrenne, Mikel 1973 *The Phenomenology of Aesthetic Experience*. Trans. from French by Edward S. Casey, *et. al.*, Evanston, IL: Northwestern University Press.

Durkheim, Émile 1951 *Suicide: A Study in Sociology*. Trans. by John A. Spaulding and George Simpson. NY: The Free Press (original 1987).

———. 1965 *The Elementary Forms of the Religious Life*. Trans. from the French by Joseph Ward Swain. NY: The Free Press (original 1915).

———. 1966 *The Rules of Sociological Method.* George E. G. Catlin, ed., trans. by Sarah A. Solovay and John H. Mueller. NY: The Free Press.

Dumézil, Georges 1988 *Mitra-Varuna: An Essay on Two Indo-European Representations of Sovereignty.* Trans. by Derek Coltman, NY: Zone Books (original 1940, revised 1948).

Duncan, James S. 1990 *The City as Text: The Politics of Landscape Interpretation in the Kandyan Kingdom.* NY: Cambridge University Press.

Dutt, Sukumar 1962 *Buddhist Monks and Monasteries of India.* London: Allen and Unwin.

Dyhrenfurth, Norman 1952 "Film Making for Scientific Field Workers," *AA,* 54:147–152.

Edgerton, Robert B. and L. L. Langness 1977 *Methods and Styles in the Study of Culture.* San Francisco: Chandler and Sharp Publishers, Inc. (original 1974).

Eggan, Dorothy 1949 "The Significance of Dreams for Anthropological Research," *AA,* 51:177–198.

Eisenberg, Leon 1977 "Disease and Illness Distinctions Between Professional and Popular Ideal of Sickness," *Culture, Medicine and Psychiatry,* 1:9–24.

Eliade, Mircea 1960 *Myths, Dreams, and Mysteries: the Encounter between contemporary Faiths and Archaic Realities.* Trans. by Philip Mairet. NY: Harper and Row.

Elsen, Albert 1967 *Purposes of Art: An Introduction to the History and Appreciation of Art.* NY: Holt, Rinehart and Winston.

Erikson, E. H. 1975 *Life History and the Historical Moment.* NY: Norton.

Evers, Hans-Dieter 1972 *Monks, Priests and Peasants: A study of Buddhism and Social Structure in Central Ceylon.* Leiden: E. J. Brill.

———. 1977 "The Social Complexity of Southeast Asian Religion: The Current Debate on Buddhism," Correspondence— *JAS,* 37(1):183–184.

Ewald, Wendy 1992 *Magic Eyes: Scenes from an Andean Girlhood.* Seattle, WA: Bay Press.

Fabrega Jr., Horacio 1978 "Ethnomedicine and Medical Science," *Medical Anthropology: Cross-cultural Studies in Health and Illness,* 2(2):11–24.

Farber, Carole 1983 "High, Healthy and Happy: Ontario Mythology on Parade," *The Celebration of Society: Perspectives on Contempo-*

rary Cultural Performance. Frank E. Manning, ed., Bowling Green, OH: Bowling Green University Popular Press, pp. 33–50.

Farber, Don 1987 *Taking Refuge in L.A.: Life in a Vietnamese Buddhist Temple.* NY: Aperture Foundation, Inc.

Ferguson, John Palmer 1975 *The Symbolic Dimensions of the Burmese Saṅgha.* Thesis *ms.,* Cornell University.

Fergusson, Francis 1949 *The Idea of a Theater: A Study of Ten Plays, The Art of Drama in Changing Perspective.* Princeton, NJ: Princeton University Press.

Fernando, Nihal and Luxshman Nadaraja 1991 *Serendip to Śrī Lankā: Im-memorial Isle.* Colombo: Studio Times Ltd., pp. 152–155.

Firth, Raymond 1934 "The Meaning of Dreams in Tikopia," *Essays Presented to C. G. Seligman.* E. E. Evans-Pritchard, Raymond Firth, Bronislow Malinowski, and Isaac Schapera, eds., London: Kegan Paul, Trench, Trubner & Co., Ltd.

Fisher, Roland 1970 "Prediction and Measurement of Perceptual-Behavioral Change in Drug-Induced Hallucination," *Origin and Mechanisms of Hallucinations.* W. Keup, ed., NY: Plenum Press.

Fong, S. L. M. 1973 "Assimilation and Changing Social Roles of Chinese Americans," *Journal of Social Issues,* 29(2):115–127.

Fox, Richard G., ed. 1991 *Recapturing Anthropology: Working in the Present.* Santa Fe, NM: School of American Research.

Frank, Gelya 1979 "Finding the Common Denominator: A Phenomeno-logical Critique of Life History Methods," *Ethos,* 7(1):68–94.

Frank, Lawrence K. 1950 *Society as the Patient: Essays on Culture and Personality.* New Brunswick, NJ: Rutgers University Press.

Freeman, James M. 1979 *Untouchable: An Indian Life History.* Stanford, CA: Stanford University Press.

Frelich, Morris, ed. 1989 *The Relevance of Culture.* NY: Bergin and Garvey Publishers.

Gandhi. 1982 (Historical drama motion picture—color) American-British-Indian production; Columbia Pictures release.

Gard, Richard 1961 *Buddhism.* NY: George Braziller.

Geertz, Clifford 1957 "Ethos, World-View and the Analysis of Sacred Symbols," *Antioch Review,* 17:421–437.

———. 1966 "Religion as a Cultural System," *Anthropological Approaches to the Study of Religion.* M. Banton, ed., ASA Monograph 3. London: Tavistock, pp. 1–46.

———. 1973 *The Interpretation of Cultures.* NY: Basic Books.

———. 1976 "Art as a Cultural System," *Modern Language Notes,* 91:1473–1499.

———. 1988 *Works and Lives: the Anthropologist as Author.* Stanford, CA: Stanford University Press.

Gellner, E. A. 1965 "Social Fact," *A Dictionary of the Social Sciences.* Julius Gould and William L. Kolb, eds., (UNESCO), NY: The Free Press, p. 655.

Globus, Gordon G. 1976 *Consciousness and the Brain: A Scientific and Philosophical Inquiry.* Gordon G. Globus, Grover Maxwell, and Irwin Savodnik, eds., NY: Plenum Press.

Gnānissara, Ven. Davuldena 1993 Personal communication.

Gnoli, Raniero 1968 *The Aesthetic Experience According to Abhinavagupta.* Varanasi: Chowkhamba Sanskrit Series.

Goffman, Erving 1982 *Interaction Ritual: Essays on Face-to-Face Behavior.* NY: Pantheon Books.

Goldenweiser, Alexander 1968 "Psychology and Culture," *History, Psychology, and Culture.* Alexander Goldenweiser, ed., Gloucester, MA: Peter Smith, pp. 59–67 (original 1923).

Goldschmidt, Walter C. 1990 *The Human Career: The Self in the Symbolic World.* Cambridge, MA: Basil Blackwell, Inc.

Gombrich, Richard F. 1971 *Precept and Practice: Traditional Buddhism in the Rural Highland of Ceylon.* Oxford: Clarendon Press.

Gombrich, Richard and Gananath Obeyesekere 1988 *Buddhism Transformed: Religious Change in Śrī Lankā.* Princeton, NJ: Princeton University Press.

Goody, Jack 1977 "Literacy and Classification: On Turning the Tables," *Text and Context: the Social Anthropology of Tradition.* Ravindra K. Jain, ed., Philadelphia: ISHI.

———. 1991 "Towards a Room with a View: A Personal Account of Contributions to Local Knowledge, Theory, and Research in Fieldwork and Comparative Studies," *Annual Review Anthropology,* 20:1–23.

Goonatileka, M. H. 1976 *The Rural Theatre and Social Satire of Śrī Lankā.* Colombo: Lake House.

Gooneratne, Yasmine 1986 *Relative Merits: A Personal Memoir of the Bandaranaike Family of Śrī Lankā*. NY: St. Martin's Press.

Goonetileke, Ian 1991 "Introduction," *Serendip to Śrī Lankā: Immemorial Isle. Fernando, Nihal and Luxshman Nadaraja*, eds., Colombo: Studio Times Limited.

Gothóni, René 1982 *Modes of Life of Theravāda Monks: A Case Study of Buddhist Monasticism in Śrī Lankā*. Studia Orientalia, 52. Helsinki: Societas Fennica.

Govinda, Lama Anagarika 1969 *The Psychological Attitude of Early Buddhist Philosophy*. NY: Samuel Weiser, Inc.

Greenholgh, Michael and Vincent Megaw, eds. 1978 *Art in Society: Studies in Style, Culture, and Aesthetics*. NY: St. Martin's Press.

Gross, Larry 1980 "Sol Worth and the Study of Visual Communications," *SAVICOM*, 6(3):2–19.

Guenther, Herbert V. 1969 *The Royal Song of Saraha: A Study in the History of Buddhist Thought*. Seattle: University of Washington Press.

Gullestad, Marianne 1993 "Autobiography by Invitation—or the Intimacy of Anonymity," presented at the panel of *Ecriture et vie privée*, conference of *Sociologie de la Lecture—Anthropologie de L'écriture. La Cité des Sciences, la Villette*, January 29th–30th.

Gunawardana, R. A. L. H. 1979 *Robe and Plough: Monasticism and Economic Interest in Early Medieval Śrī Lankā*. Monographs of the Association for Asian Studies, 35. Tucson: University of Arizona Press.

Halsey, Margaret 1963 *The Pseudo-Ethic*. NY: Simon and Schuster.

Hanneman, Yvonne 1973 *The Work of Gomis*. A film that records the ceremonies of Gomis who practices healing in the Southern Province of Śrī Lankā.

Harring, Douglas G. 1956 *Personal Character and Cultural Milieu*. Syracuse: Syracuse University Press.

Harris, Theodore F. 1969 *Pearl S. Buck: A Biography*. NY: The John Day Co., Inc.

——. 1971 *Pearl S. Buck: Her Philosophy as Expressed in Her Letters*. NY: The John Day Co., Inc.

Harvey, Peter 1990 *An Introduction to Buddhism: Teachings, History, and Practices*. NY: Cambridge University Press.

Harvey, Youngsook Kim 1979 *Six Korean Women: The Socialization of Shamans*. St. Paul: West Publishing Co.

Hayashima, Kyosho 1969 "The Character of Theravāda Buddhism with special reference to Ceylonese Buddhism," *Religion and Politics in Southeast Asia.* Taysuro Yamamoto, ed.

Hazra, Kanai Lal 1982 *History of Theravāda Buddhism in South-East Asia with Special Reference to India and Ceylon.* New Delhi: Munshiram Manoharlal Publishers Pvt. Ltd.

Heider, Karl G. 1976 *Ethnographic Film.* Austin: University of Texas Press.

———. 1991 "Are Indonesian Films Really Indonesian?" *Visual Anthropology,* 4(1):53–55.

Hendrickson, Paul 1979 "Rosemary Rogers: The Princess of Passion Pulp," Colombo, *The Sunday Times,* July 15th, p. 8.

Hitchcock, Jonh T. and J. Patricia 1960 "Some Considerations for the Prospective Ethnographic Cinematographer," *AA,* 62:656–674.

Hockings, Paul, ed. 1975 *Principles of Visual Anthropology.* The Hague: Mouton and Company.

Holt, John Clifford 1991 *Buddha in the Crown: Avalokieśvara in the Buddhist Traditions of Śrī Lankā.* NY: Oxford University Press.

Homans, George C. 1967 *The Nature of Social Science.* NY: Harcourt, Brace & World.

Honigmann, John J. 1976 "The Personal Approach in Cultural Anthropological Research," *Current Anthropology,* 17(2):243–261.

Hospers, John 1969 *Introductory Readings in Aesthetics.* NY: The Free Press.

Hsu, Francis L. K. 1961 *Psychological Anthropology: Approaches to Culture and Personality.* Homewood, IL: The Dorsey Press (revised 1972).

Hughes, H. Stuart 1958 *Consciousness and Society.* NY: Vintage Books.

Humphreys, Christmas 1956 *A Buddhist Student's Manual.* London: Buddhist Society.

Husmann, Rolf, Ingrid Wellinger, Johnnes Rühl, and Martin Taureg, eds. 1993 *A Bibliography of Ethnographic Film.* Association for International Scientific Communications, Göttingen, Germany. Hamburg: LIT-Verlag. Boulder, CO: Westview Press.

Huxley, Aldous 1954 *The Doors of Perception.* NY: Harper.

Independence Vesak 1947 An issue which includes the "Pageant of Śrī Lankā," Colombo.

Ikeda, Daisaku 1976 *The Living Buddha: An Interpretive Biography.* Trans. by Burton Watson. NY: Weatherhill.

Inkeles, Alex 1975 "Becoming Modern: Individual Change in Six Developing Countries," *Ethos*, 3(2):323–342.

James, William 1960 *The Varieties of Religious Experience.* London.

Jarvie, I. C. 1976 "On the Limits of Symbolic Interpretation in Anthropology," *Current Anthropology*, 17(4):687–701.

The Jātaka or Stories of the Buddha's Former Births 1957 E. B. Cowell, ed., trans. by H. T. Francis and W. H. D. Rouse. Pāli Text Society. London: Luzac and Company, Ltd.

Jayasuriya, W. F. 1963 *The Psychology and Philosophy of Buddhism.* Colombo: YMBA Press.

Jayatilleke, K. N. 1963 *Early Buddhist Theory of Knowledge.* London: Allen-Unwin.

Johnston, E. H. 1978 *Aśvaghoṣa's Buddhacarita or Acts of the Buddha.* Delhi: Motilal Banarsidass (original 1936).

Jouveau-Dubreuil, G. 1937 *Iconography of Southern India.* Paris: Librairie Orientaliste Paul Geuthner.

Joyce, James 1961 *Ulysses.* NY: Random House (original 1922).

Kabilsingh, Chatsumarn 1988 "Buddhist Education on Conservation," presentation for the *6th International Conference on Buddhist Education*, Institute for Sino-Indian Buddhist Studies, Taipei.

Kale, M. R. 1924 *Bāṇa's Kādambarī.* Bombay: Vāman Yashvant and Co.

Kalupahana, David J. 1976 *Buddhist Philosophy: A Historical Analysis.* Honolulu: University Press of Hawaii.

Kapferer, Bruce 1975 *Form and Transformation in Ritual Performance: The Organization of Emotion and Feeling in Sinhalese Healing Rites*, presentation for the Symposium: The Work of Ritual: Time, Motion and Emotion, at the *Annual Meeting of the American Anthropological Association*, San Francisco.

——. 1977 "First Class to Maradana: Secular Drama in Sinhalese Healing Rites," *Secular Ritual*, Sally F. Moore and Barbara G. Myerhoff, eds., Assen/Amsterdam: Van Gorcum, pp. 91–123.

——. 1983 *A Celebration of Demons: Exorcism and the Aesthetics of Healing in Śrī Laṅkā.* Bloomington: Indiana University Press.

——. 1988   *Legends of People: Myths of State.* Washington, DC: Smithsonian Institution Press.

——. 1989   "Nationalist Ideology and a Comparative Anthropology," presetation for sub-theme I: Cultural Exchange and Cultural Nationalism, *The Seoul Olympiad Anniversary Conference*, Seoul.

Kardiner, A. 1939   *The Individual and His Society.* NY: Columbia University Press.

Karim, Wazir Jahan, ed. 1990   *Emotions of Culture: A Malay Perspective* NY: Oxford University Press.

Karunaratne, L. K. 1948   "Sittara Painting," *A Collection of Ceylon Frescoes Depicting Jātaka Stories.* Ceylon Daily News Vesak Number.

Kataragama—A God for All Seasons.   1973   Anthropologist: Gananath Obeyesekere, motion picture by Granada Television.

Katz, John   1978   *Anthropology: Film/Video/Photograph.* Art Gallery of Ontario, Canada.

Kemper, Steven E. G.   1979   "Sinhalese Astrology, South Asia Caste Systems, and the Notion of Individuality," *JAS*, 38(3):477–497

——. 1980   "Reform and Segmentation in Monastic Fraternities in Low Country Śrī Lankā," *JAS*, 40(1):27–41.

Kennedy, John G.   1969   "Psychosocial Dynamics of Witchcraft Systems," *International Journal of Social Psychiatry*, 15(3):165–178.

Keyes, Charles F. 1983   "Merit-Transference in the Kammic Theory of Popular Theravāda Buddhism," *Karma: An Anthropological Inquiry.* Charles F. Keyes and E. Valentine Daniel, eds., Berkeley: UC Press, pp. 261–286

Kikumura, Akemi 1981   *Through Harsh Winters: The Life of a Japanese Immigrant Woman.* Novato, CA: Chandler and Sharp Publishers, Inc.

Kindered Sayings.   1917   London: Pāli Text Society, p. 25.

Kingston, Maxine Hong 1977   *The Woman Warrior.* NY: Vintage Books.

Kirsch, A. Thomas 1977   "Complexity in the Thai Religious System: An Interpretation," *JAS*, 36(2):241–266.

Klausner, William J. 1964   "Popular Buddhism in Northeast Thailand," *Cross-Cultural Understanding: Epistemology in Anthropology.* F. S. C. Northrop and Helen H. Livingston, eds., NY: Harper and Row, pp. 70–92.

Kluckhohn, Clyde 1949 "Personality in Culture (The Individual and the Group)," *Mirror for Man: The Relation of Anthropology to Modern Life.* Clyde Kluckhohn, ed., NY: McGraw-Hill, pp. 196–261.

Knox, Robert 1911 *An Historical Relation of Ceylon* together with Somewhat Concerning Severall Remarkeable Passages of my Life that Hath Hapned Since my deliverance out of my Captivity. Glasgow: J. MacLehose and Sons (original 1681).

Kotelawala, Sir John 1956 *An Asian Prime Minister's Story.* London: George G. Harrap and Co. Ltd.

Kuper, Adam 1979 "The Structure of Dreams," *Man,* 14(4):645–662.

Kuper, Hilda 1978 *Sobhuza II, Ngwenyama and King of Swaziland: The Story of an Hereditary Ruler of His Country.* NY: Holmes and Meier Publishers, Inc. (Africana Publishing Company).

———. 1982 Seminar communication.

Kwai, Tung-lin and Tung-hsin Lun 1988 "Buddhist T'sung-lin (Forest) Education and the Preservation of the Nature Environment," presented at the *6th International Conference on Buddhist Education,* Institute for Sino-Indian Buddhist Studies, Taipei.

LaFleur, William 1979 "Points of Departure: Comments on Religious Pilgrimage in Śrī Lankā and Japan," *JAS,* 38(2):271–181.

Laing, Ronald D. 1970 *Knots.* NY: Pantheon.

Lambrecht, Frank L. 1975 "Fishing Crafts of Ceylon," *Oceans,* January: 13–19.

Langness, L. L. 1965 *The Life History in the Anthropological Science.* NY: Holt, Rinehart and Winston.

———. 1977 "Counting Coups," a chapter excerpted from Peter Nabokov (1967), in his *Other Fields, Other Grasshoppers: Readings in Cultural Anthropology.* NY: J. B. Lippincott Co., pp. 61–72.

Langness, L. L. and Gelya Frank 1978 "Fact, Fiction and the Ethnographic Novel," *Anthropology and Humanism Quarterly,* 3(1–2):18–22.

———. 1981 *Lives: An Anthropological Approach to Biography.* Novato, CA: Chandler and Sharp Publishers, Inc.

Laski, M. 1961 *Ecstasy: A Study of Some Secular and Religious Experiences.* London: Cresset Press.

Leach, E. R. 1961 *Pul Eliya, A Village in Ceylon: A Study of Land Tenure and Kinship.* London: Cambridge University Press.

———. 1962 "Pulleyar and the Lord Buddha: An Aspect of Religious Syn-
cretism in Ceylon," *Psycho-Analysis and the Psycho-Analytic Review*,
49(2).

Leacock, Richard 1975 "Ethnographic Observation and the Super-8 Mil-
limeter Camera," *Principles of Visual Anthropology*. Paul Hockings,
ed., Chicago: Aldine Publishing Co.

Lerner, Eric 1977 *Journey of Insight Meditation*. NY: Schoken Books.

Leslie, Charles ed. 1976 *Asian Medical Systems: A Comparative Study*.
Berkeley: UC Press.

Lessa, William A. and Evon Z. Vogt 1979 *Reader in Comparative Religion: An Anthropological Approach*. NY: Harper and Row.

Lester, Robert C. 1973 *Theravāda Buddhism in Southeast Asia*. Ann
Arbor: University of Michigan Press, see pp. 83–108, 109–129.

Levy, Mervyn 1958 "Honesty and Distortion in Creative Photography,"
Photograms 1958. London: Iliffe.

Lewis, I. M. 1978 *An Anthropological Study of Spirit Possession and
Shamanism*. NY: Penguin Books.

Li, You-Yi 1982 Seminar communication.

Lifton, Robert Jay, and Shuichi Kato, and Michael R. Reich 1979 *Six Lives,
Six Deaths: Portraits from Modern Japan*. New Haven, CT: Yale
University Press.

Lincoln, Bruce 1981 *Priests, Warriors, and Cattle: A Study in the Ecology
of Religions*. Berkeley: UC Press.

Littleton, Scott 1966 *The New Comparative Mythology: An Anthropological Assessment of the Theories of Georges Dumézil*. Berkeley: UC
Press.

Loizos, Peter 1980 "Granada Television's Disappearing World Series: An
Appraisal," *AA*, 82:573–594.

Lommel, Andreas 1972 "Ceylon," *Masks: Their Meaning and Function*.
Trans. by Nadia Fowler. London: Paul Elek, pp. 77–92.

Loofs, H. H. E. 1975 "The Significance of Changing Perceptions of the
Buddha Image in Mainland Southeast Asia for the Understanding of
the Individual's Place in Some Buddhist Societies," *Self and Biography: Essays on the Individual and Society in Asia*. Gungwu Wang,
ed., Sydney: Sydney University Press.

Ludwig, Arnold 1968 "Altered States of Conciousness," *Trance and Possessions States*. Raymond Prince, ed., Montreal: R. M. Bucke Society.

MacAloon, John J. 1981 *This Great Symbol.* Chicago: University of Chicago Press.

MacLuhan, Marshall 1964 *Understanding Media: The Extensions of Man.* NY: McGraw-Hill.

Mahāvamsa. Geiger-Bode version of 1912, Colombo: Ceylon Government Information Department, 1950.

Malalasekera, George P. 1958 *The Pāli Literature of Ceylon.* Colombo: M. D. Gunasena.

Malalgoda, Kitsiri 1976 *Buddhism in Sinhalese Society, 1750–1900: A Study of Religious Revival and Change.* Berkeley: UC Press.

Malaviya, Debi Prasad 1958 *Nalopākhyāna,* with English Translation. Allahabad: Ram Narainlal.

Malle, Louis 1970 *Phantom India—Reflections on a Voyage.* Eight part documentary of the film maker's impressions of India.

Maloney, Clarence 1974a *Peoples of South Asia.* NY: Holt, Rinehart and Winston.

———. 1974b *South Asia: Seven Community Profiles.* NY: Holt, Rinehart and Winston.

Mandelbaum, David G. 1964 "Introduction: Process and Structure in South Asian Religion," *JAS,* 23 (June):5–20.

———. 1973 "The Study of Life History: Gandhi," *Current Anthropology.* 14:177–206.

Manning, Frank E. 1983 *The Celebration of Society: Perspectives on Contemporary Cultural Performance.* Bowling Green, OH: Bowling Green University Popular Press, pp. 1–30.

Manogaran, Chelvadurai 1987 *Ethnic Conflict and Reconcilation in Śrī Lankā.* Honolulu: University of Hawaii Press.

Maquet, Jacques 1964a "Some Epistemological Remarks on the Cultural Philosophies and Their Comparison," *Cross-Cultural Understanding: Epistemology in Anthropology.* F. S. C. Northrop and Helen H. Livingston, eds., NY: Harper and Row, pp. 13–31.

———. 1964b "Objectivity in Anthropology," *Current Anthropology,* 5(1):47–55.

———. 1971 *Power and Society in Africa.* NY: McGraw-Hill.

———. 1975a "Expressive Space and Theravāda Values: A Meditation Monastery in Śrī Lankā," *Ethos,* 3(1):1–21.

———. 1975b "Meditation in Contemporary Śrī Lankā: Idea and Practice," *The Journal of Transpersonal Psychology*, 7(2):182–196.

———. 1979 *Introduction to Aesthetic Anthropology*. Malibu: Undena.

———. 1986 *Aesthetic Experience: An Anthropologist Looks at the Visual Arts*. NY: Yale University Press.

Marshall, John, Adrienne Miesmer, and Sue Marshall Cabezas 1980 *N!ai, The Story of a !Kung Woman*. Originally aired in the Odyssey series, motion picture, 59 mins., available from Documentary Educational Resources, Watertown, MA, USA.

Martin, F. David 1972 *Art and The Religious Experience: The "Language" of the Sacred*. Lewisburg, PA: Bucknell University Press.

Maruyama, Magoroh 1974 "Symbiotization of Cultural Heterogeneity: Scientific Epistemological and Esthetic Bases," *Co-Existence*, 11:42–56.

Maruyama, Magoroh and Arthur M. Harkins, eds. 1978 *Cultures of the Future*, World Anthropology Series, Beresford BK Serv.

Maslow, Abraham H. 1981 *Religious, Values, and Peak-experiences*. NY: Penguin Books.

Masson, J. Moussaieff 1976 "The Psychology of the Ascetic," *JAS*, 35 (4):611-625.

May, Rollo 1953 *Man's Search for Himself*. NY: W.W. Norton & Co.

McAlpine, W. R. 1980 *A Vesak Oratorio: The Birth, Enlightenment and Passing Away of the Buddha*. Colombo: Lake House.

McCabe, Joseph 1912 *Twelve Years in a Monastery*. London: Watts and Company.

McGill, Gary 1982 Personal communication.

Mead, Margaret 1970 "The Art and Technology of Field Work," *A Handbook of Method in Cultural Anthropology*. Radul Naroll and Ronald Cohen, eds., Garden City, NY: The Natural History Press, pp. 246–265.

Mead, Margaret and Frances Cook MacGregor 1951 *Growth and Culture: A Photographic Study of Balinese Childhood*. NY: P.G. Putnam's Sons.

Meagher, Robert E. 1977 "Strangers at the Gate: Ancient Rites of Hospitality," *Parabola*, 2(4):10–15.

Meegaskumbura, Punchi Banda 1983 Personal communication.

Merriam, Alan P. 1964 "The Arts and Anthropology" *Horizons of Anthropology*, Sol Tax, ed., Chicago: Aldine, pp. 224–236.

Michaelis, Anthony R. 1955 *Research Films in Biology, Anthropology, Psychology, and Medicine.* NY: Academic Press.

Milton, John R. 1971 *Conversations with Frank Waters.* Chicago: Sage Books.

Moerman, Michael 1966 "Ban Ping's Temple: The Center of a 'Loosely Structured' Society," *Anthropological Studies in Theravāda Buddhism.* M. Nash, ed., Cultural Report Series, 13 (Yale University Southeast Asia Studies) pp. 137–174.

Moore, Sally Falk 1975 "Epilogue: Uncertainties in Situations, Indeterminacies in Culture," *Symbol and Politics in Communal Ideology: Cases and Questions*, S. F. Moore and B. G. Myerhoff, eds., Ithaca, NY: Cornell University Press, pp. 210–219.

——. 1980 Seminar communication.

Myerhoff, Barbara with Deena Metzger, Jay Ruby, and Virginia Tufte 1992 *Remembered Lives: The Work of Ritual, Storytelling, and Growing Older.* Marc Kaminsky, ed., Ann Arbor: University of Michigan Press.

Nabokov, Peter 1967 *Two Leggings: The Making of a Crow Warrior.* NY: Thomas Y. Crowell Co.

Narada Thera, Ven. 1964 *The Buddha and His Teachings.* Colombo: Vajirarama.

Nash, Manning 1966 "Introduction," *Anthropological Studies in Theravāda Buddhism.* M. Nash, ed., Cultural Report Series, 13 (Yale University Southeast Asia Studies) pp. vii–xii.

Needham, Rodney 1978 *Primordial Characters.* Charlottesville: University of Virginia Press.

Norman Jr., Wilbert Reuben 1991 "Photography as a Research Tool," *Visual Anthropology*, 4(2):193–216.

Nyanaponika Thera, Ven. 1975 *The Heart of Buddhist Meditation.* NY: Samuel Weiser (original 1962).

Nyanatiloka, Ven. 1972 *Buddhist Dictionary: Manual of Buddhist Terms and Doctrines.* Colombo: Frewin and Co., Ltd. (original 1952).

Obeyesekere, Gananath 1958 "The Structure of Sinhalese Ritual," *Ceylon Journal of Historical and Social Studies*, 1:192–202.

——. 1966 "The Buddhist Pantheon in Ceylon and its Extensions," *Anthropological Studies in Theravāda Buddhism.* M. Nash, ed., Cultural Report Series, 13 (Yale University Southeast Asia Studies) pp. 1–26.

——. 1969 "The Ritual Drama of the Sanni Demons: Collective Representations of Disease in Ceylon," *Comparative Studies in Society and History,* 11.

——. 1972 "Religious Symbolism and Political Change in Ceylon," *The Two Wheels of Dhamma: Essays on the Theravāda Tradition in India and Ceylon.* Gananath Obeyesekere, Frank Reynolds, and Bardwell Smith, eds., Chambersburg, PA: American Academy of Religion, 3:58–78.

——. 1975 "Sinhalese-Buddhist Identity in Ceylon," *Ethnic Identity: Cultural Continuities and Change.* George De Vos and Lola Romanucci-Ross, eds., Palo Alto, CA: Mayfield.

——. 1976 "The Impact of Ayurvedic Ideas on the Culture and the Individual in Śrī Lankā," *Asian Medical Systems: A Comparative Study.* Charles Leslei, ed., Berkeley: UC Press.

——. 1979 "The Fire-walkers of Kataragama: The Rise of *Bhakti* Religiosity in Buddhist Śrī Lankā," *JAS,* 37(3):457–476.

——. 1981 *Medusa's Hair: An Essay on Personal Symbols and Religious Experience.* Chicago: University of Chicago Press.

——. 1984 *The Cult of the Goddess Pattini.* Chicago: University of Chicago Press.

——. 1990 *The Work of Culture: Symbolic Transformation in Psychoanalysis and Anthropology.* Chicago: University of Chicago Press.

Obeyesekere, Ranjini 1990 "The Significance of Performance for its Audience: An Analysis of Three Śrī Lankā Rituals," *By Means of Performance: Intercultural Studies of Theatre and Ritual.* Richard Schechner and Willa Appel, eds., NY: Cambridge University Press, pp. 118–130.

Obeyesekere, Ranjini and Chitra Fernando, eds. 1981 *An Anthology of Modern Writing from Śrī Lankā.* Association for Asian Studies Monograph, 38, Tucson: University of Arizona Press.

Ohrn, Steven and Michael E. Bell, eds., 1975 *Saying Cheese: Studies in Folklore and Visual Communication.* Folklore Forum, a communication for students of Folklore, Bibliographic and Special Series, 13.

Okely, Judith and Helen Callaway, eds. 1992 *Anthropology and Autobiography.* ASA Monograph, 29. London: Routledge.

Oman, John Campbell 1903 *The Mystics, Ascetics, and Saints of India: A Study of Sadhuism, with an Account of the Yogis, Sanyasis, Bairagis, and Other Strange Hindu Sectarians.* London: T. Fisher Unwin.

Ornstein, Robert E. 1973a *The Nature of Human Consciousness: A Book of Readings.* San Francisco: W. H. Freeman and Co.

———. 1973b *The Psychology of Consciousness.* San Francisco: W. H. Freeman and Co.

Ortega y Gasset, Jose 1972 *The Dehumanization of Art, and other Essays on Art, Culture, and Literature.* Princeton, NJ: Princeton University Press.

Paranavitana, S. 1929 "Pre-Buddhist Religious Beliefs in Ceylon," *Journal of Royal Asiatic Society* (Ceylon Branch), 31(82): 302–327.

———. 1954 *Art and Architecture of Ceylon: Polonnaruva Period.* Colombo: The Arts Council of Ceylon.

———. 1958 *The God of Adam's Peak.* Ascona: Artibus Asiae.

———. 1967 *Sinhalayo.* Colombo: Lake House.

———. 1988 *The Stupa in Celyon.* Memoirs of the Archaeological Survey of Ceylon, 5, Colombo Museum (original 1946, Ceylon Government Press).

Pathamasamajīvī Suttam. 1885 *Aṅguttara Nikāya*, vol. 2 (Catukkaniāta) p. 61. Edited by Richard Morris. London: Pāli Text Society.

Payne, Richard K. 1991 "Early Buddhism: A Conversation with David J. Kalupahana," *The Pacific World*, Journal of the Institude of Buddhist Studies, New Series, 7 (Fall): 94–95.

Peacock, Olive 1989 *Minority Politics in Śrī Lankā (A Study of the Burghers).* Jiapur, India: Arihant Publishers.

Pelto, P. J. 1970 *Anthropological Research: The Structure of Inquiry.* NY: Harper & Row.

Pertold, Otaker 1973 *Ceremonial Dances of the Sinhalese.* Dehiwala, Śrī Lankā: Tisara Press.

Peters, Larry 1981 *Ecstacy and Healing in Nepal.* Malibu, CA: Undena.

Pfanner, D. E. 1966 "The Buddhist Monk in Rural Burmese Society," *Anthropological Studies in Theravāda Buddhism.* M. Nash, ed., Cultural Report Series, 13 (Yale University Southeast Asia Studies) pp. 94–95.

Pike, K. 1954 *Language in Relation to a Unified Theory of the Structure of Human Behavior*, 1. Glendale, CA: Summer Institute of Linguistics.

Postel-Coster, Els 1977 "The Indonesian Novel as a Source of Anthropological Data," *Text and Context*. Ravindra K. Jain, ed., Philadelphia: ISHI.

Powdermaker, Hortense 1966 *Stranger and Friend: The Way of an Anthropologist*. NY: Norton.

Preloran, Jorge 1975 "Documenting the Human Condition," *Principles of Visual Anthropology*. Paul Hockings, ed., The Hague: Mouton, pp. 103–107.

Presler, Franklin A. 1987 *Religion Under Bureaucracy Policy and Administration for Hindu Temples in South India*. NY: Cambridge University Press.

Prince, Raymond H. 1974 "The Problem of 'Spirit Possession' as a Treatment for Psychiatric Disorders," *Ethos*, 2(4):315–333.

Price-Williams, Douglass 1975 *Explorations in Cross-Cultural Psychology*. San Francisco: Chandler and Sharp Publishers, Inc.

Professional Ethics: Statements and Procedures of the American Anthropological Association. 1973 Washington, DC.

Rabinow, Paul 1982 "Masked I Go Forward," *A Crack in the Mirror: Reflexive Perspectives in Anthropology*, Jay Ruby, ed., Philadelphia: University of Pennsylvania Press, pp. 173–185.

Radin, Paul 1913 "Personal Reminiscences of a Winnebago Indian," *Journal of American Folklore*, 26:293–318.

——. 1920 *The Autobiography of a Winnebago Indian*. UC Publications in American Archaeology and Ethnology, 16(7):381–473.

——. 1926 *Crashing Thunder: The Autobiography of an American Indian*. NY: Appleton.

——. 1957 *Primitive Man as Philosopher*. NY: Dover.

Raghaven, M. D. 1962 *Ceylon: A Pictorial Survey of the People and Arts*. Colombo: M. D. Gunasena.

Rahula, Ven. Walpola 1956 *The History of Buddhism in Ceylon*. Colombo: M. D. Gunasena.

——. 1959 *What the Buddha Taught*. NY: Grove Press.

Ramanujan, A. K. 1973 *Speaking of Śiva*. Baltimore, MD: Penguin Books.

Ratanasara, Ven. Havanpola 1972 *Britānya Pratipatti Budu Samaya Hā Piriven Adhyāpanaya 1815–1965*. Kelaniya, Śrī Lankā: Deepa Press (English edition 1965).

Ratnapala, Nandasena 1991 *Folklore of Śrī Lankā.* Colombo: The State Printing Corporation, Śrī Lankā.

Ravičz, Marilyn Ekdahl 1974 *Aesthetic Anthropology: Theory and Analysis of Pop and Conceptual Art in America.* Ph.D. dissertation *ms.*, Department of Anthropology, UCLA.

Read, Herbert 1976 *To Hell with Culture, and Other Essays on Art and Society.* NY: Schocken Books (original 1963).

Redfield, Robert 1956 *Peasant Society and Culture.* Chicago: University of Chicago Press.

Reed, Stanley 1970 "The Film-maker and the Audience," *The Social Context of Art.* Jean Creedy, ed., London: Tavistock Publications, pp. 127–146.

Reynolds, Christopher, ed. 1970 *An Anthology of Sinhalese Literature—Up to 1815.* London: George Allen & Unwin Ltd.

Reynolds, Craig J. 1976 "Buddhist Cosmography in Thai History, with Special Reference to Nineteenth-Century Culture Change," *JAS,* 36(2): 203–220.

Rhys Davids, Mrs. (Caroline Augusta Foley) 1941 *Poems of Cloister and Jungle: A Buddhist Anthology.* London: Pāli Text Society, John Murray.

——. 1964 *Psalms of the Early Buddhists: I. The Sisters, II. The Brethren.* London: Pāli Text Society, Luzac and Company.

Rhys Davids, T. W. 1880 *Jātakas: Buddhist Birth Stories, or Jātaka Tales.* Boston: Houghton, Miffin, and Co.

Riesman, Paul 1977 *Freedom in Fulani Social Life: An Introspective Ethnography.* Chicago: University of Chicago Press.

Rittenberg, W. 1977 "How to Describe a Ceremony," presented at the *Annual Meetings of the American Anthropological Association,* Houston, Texas.

Robinson, Richard and Willard Johnson 1977 *The Buddhist Religion.* Encino, CA: Dickenson Publishing Co., Inc.

Roheim, Geza 1969 *Psychoanalysis and Anthropology.* NY: International University.

Rollwagen, Jack R., ed. 1992 *Anthropological Filmmaking: Anthropological Perspectives on the Production of Film and Video for General Public Audiences.* Chur: Harwood Academic Publishers (original 1988).

Rose, Dan 1982 "Occasions and Forms of the Anthropological Experience," *A Crack in the Mirror: Reflexive Perspectives in Anthropology.* Jay Ruby, ed., Philadelphia: University of Pennsylvania Press, pp. 219–273.

Rosenthal, Bernard Gordon 1971 *The Images of Man.* NY: Basic Books.

Rouch, Jean 1975 "The Camera and Man," *Principles of Visual Anthropology,* Paul Hockings, ed., Chicago: Aldine Publishing Co., pp. 83–102.

Ruby, Jay 1977 "The Image Mirrored: Reflexivity and the Documentary Film," *Journal of the University Film Association,* 29(1).

——. 1988 Personal communication.

Ruddock, Ralph 1972 "Conditions of Personal Identity," *Six Approaches to the Person.* Ralph Ruddock, ed., London: Routledge and Kegan Paul, pp. 93–125.

Rundstrom, Don 1992 "Imaging Anthropology," *Anthropological Filmmaking: Anthropological Perspectives on the Production of Film and Video for General Public Audiences.* Jack R. Rollwagen, ed., Chur: Harwood Academic Publishers (original 1988), pp. 317–370.

Rundstrom, Don, Ron Rundstrom, and Clinton Bergum 1973 *Japanese Tea: The Aesthetics, The Way: An Ethnographic Companion to the Film—The Path* (1971 Sumai Film Company). Andover, MA: Warner Modular Publications Inc.

Ryan, Bryce 1958 *Sinhalese Village.* Miami: University of Miami Press.

Ryder, Elizabeth Lee 1992 *Iambakey Okuk: Interpretations of a Lifetime of Change in Papua New Guinea.* Ph.D. dissertation *ms.,* Department of Anthropology, UCLA.

Samarasinhe, D. M. 1957 *Kādamabarī.* Colombo: Ratnākara Book Depot.

Samyutta Nikāya (Grouped Suttas). 1884 London: Pāli Text Society.

Sarathchandra, E. R. 1953 *The Sinhalese Folk Play and the Modern Stage.* Colombo: Ceylon University Press.

——. 1958 *Buddhist Psychology of Perception.* Colombo: Lake House Press.

——. 1966 *The Folk Drama of Ceylon.* Ceylon Department of Cultural Affairs.

Sarada, Ven. Weragoda 1991 *Life of the Buddha in Pictures.* Sinhala/English, Chinese/English, (Japanese/English 1993). Singapore: The Singapore Buddhist Meditation Centre.

Sartre, Jean-Paul 1964 *Nausea*. Trans. by Lloyd Alexander. NY: New Directions.

Saverimuttu, Renee Catherine 1971 *The Development of the Sinhalese Cinema: A Historical Survey of Films and Personalities from 1947–1967 Taking into Account Past Trends and Future Possibilities*. Thesis *ms.*, Department of Theater Arts, UCLA.

Sawada, Noriko 1980 "Memoir of a Japanese Daughter," *Ms.*, April.

Sax, William S. 1991 *Mountain Goddess: Gender and Politics in a Himalayan Pilgrimage*. NY: Oxford University Press.

Schapiro, Meyer 1953 "Style," *Anthropology Today*. A. L. Kroeber, ed., Chicago: University of Chicago Press.

Schecter, Jerrold 1967 *The New Face of Buddha: Buddhism and Political Power in Southeast Asia*. Tokyo: John Weatherhill, Inc.

Schechner, Richard 1990 "Magnitudes of Performance," *By Means of Performance: Intercultural Studies of Theatre and Ritual*. Richard Schechner and Willa Appel, eds., NY: Cambridge University Press, pp. 19–49.

Schechner, Richard and Willa Appel, eds. 1990 *By Means of Performance: Intercultural Studies of Theatre and Ritual*. NY: Cambridge University Press.

Schelfen, Albert E. 1973 *Body Language and the Social Order: Communication as Behavioral Control*. Englewood Cliffs, NJ: Prentice-Hall.

Schutz, Alfred 1967 *The Phenomenology of the Social World*. Trans. by George Walsh and Frederick Lehnert. Evanston, IL: Northwestern University Press (original 1932).

Seaton, S. Lee and Karen Ann Watson-Gego 1978 "Meta-Anthro-pology: The Elementary Forms of Ethnological Thought," in their ed. *Adaptation and Symbolism* dedicated to Raymond Firth. Honolulu: East-West Center Press, pp. 173–218.

Seligmann, C. G. 1909 "Note on the 'Bandar' Cult of the Kandyan Sinhalese," *Man*, 9(77):130–134.

———. 1923 "Notes on Dreams," *Man* 23:186–188.

Seligmann, C. G. and B. Z. Seligmann 1911 *The Veddās*. Cambridge: Cambridge University Press.

Seneviratna, Anurādha 1992 *The Buddha Śākyamuni*. Colombo: Associated Newspapers of Ceylon Limited.

Seneviratne, H. L. 1961 "Vihāraya, Devālaya hā Sinhala Samājaya," *Sanskruti*, 9(1):25–29.

———. 1963 "The Äsala Perahära in Kandy," *Ceylon Journal of Historical and Social Studies*, 6(2):169–180.

———. 1970 "The Sacred and the Profane in a Buddhist Rite," *Ceylon Studies Seminar Series* ('69/'70),7.

———. 1977 "Review of *Monks, Priests and Peasants*, by Hans-Dieter Evers," *JAS*, 36(1).

———. 1978 *Rituals of the Kandyan State*. NY: Cambridge University Press.

Sharon, Douglas G. 1978 *Wizard of the Four Winds*. NY: The Free Press.

Shelston, Alan 1977 *Biography*. NY: Harper.

Shostak, Marjorie 1983 *Nisa: The Life and Words of a !Kung Woman*. NY: Random House (original 1981).

Simon, Herbert Alexander 1969 *The Sciences of the Artificial*. Cambridge, MA: MIT Press.

Simons, Ronald C. 1973 *Floating in the Air, Followed by the Wind: Thaipusam: A Hindu Festival*. A film distributed by Indiana University, Audio-Visual Center.

Singer, Milton 1961 "A Survey of Culture and Personality Theory and Research," *Studying Personality Cross-Culturally*. Bert Kaplan, ed., Evanston, IL: Harper & Row, Publishers, pp. 9–90.

Smart, Ninian 1973a *The Phenomenon of Religion*. NY: Herder and Herder.

———. 1973b *The Science of Religion and The Sociology of Knowledge: Some Methodological Questions*. Princeton, NJ: Princeton University Press.

Soni, R. L. 1945 *Buddhism: My Conception of It*. Calcutta: Mahā Bodhi Society Publication.

Sontag, Susan 1980 *On Photography*. NY: Delta Book.

Sorata, Ven. P. 1979 *Ven. Hanchāpola Śrī Gnānavansa Thero: The Life History of a Śrī Lankā Headmonk*. A short account taken from my research for the headmonk's funeral.

Sorenson, E. Richard 1974 "Anthropological Film: A Scientific and Humanistic Resource," *Science*, 186(4169):1079–1085.

Southwold, Martin 1978 "Definition and Its Problems in Social Anthropology," *The Year-Book of Symbolic Anthropology*. I. E. Schwimmer, ed., London: C. Hurst.

———. 1979a "Buddhism and the Definition of Religion," *Man*, 13(3):362–379.

———. 1979b "Religious Belief," *Man*, 14(4):628–644.

———. 1982 "True Buddhism and Village Buddhism in Śrī Lankā," *Religious Organization and Religious Experience*. John Davis, ed., NY: Academic Press.

———. 1983 *Buddhism in Life: The Anthropological study of Religion and the Sinhalese Practice of Buddhism*. Manchester: Manchester University Press.

Spencer, Robert F. 1966 "Ethical Expression in a Burmese Jātaka," *The Anthropologist Looks at Myth*. Melville Jacobs and John Greenway, eds., University of Texas Press, published for the American Folklore Society, 17.

Spiro, Melford E. 1965 *Context and Meaning in Cultural Anthropology*. In honor of A. I. Hallowell. NY: The Free Press.

———. 1966 "Religion: Problems of Definition and Explanation," *Anthropological Approaches to the Study of Religion*. M. Banton, ed., London: Tavistock, pp. 93–94.

———. 1967 *Burmese Supernaturalism*. Englewood Cliffs, NJ: Prentice-Hall.

———. 1968 "Culture and Personality," *International Encyclopedia of the Social Sciences*, 3. D. L. Sills, ed., NY: Crowell, Collier and Macmillan, Inc., pp. 558–563.

———. 1970 *Buddhism and Society: A Great Tradition and Its Burmese Vicissitudes*. NY: Harper and Row.

———. 1977 *Kinship and Marriage in Burma: A Cultural and Psychodynamic Analysis*. Berkeley: UC Press.

———. 1987 *Culture and Human Nature: Theoretical Papers of Melford E. Spiro*. Benjamin Kilborne and L. L. Langness, eds., Chicago: University of Chicago Press.

Spradley, James P. 1980 *Participant Observation*. NY: Holt, Rinehart and Winston.

Śrī Lankā Department of Census and Statistics 1981 Colombo: Śrī Lankā Government Printing.

Stace, Walter 1973 "The Nature of Mysticism," *Philosophy of Religion*, William L. Rowe, ed., NY: Harcourt Brace Jovanovich, Inc., pp. 264–279.

Stravinsky, Igor and Robert Craft 1960 *Memories and Commentaries*. Berkeley: UC Press.

Strecker, Ivo 1982 "The Short Take," *RAIN*, 50:10–12.

Streng, Frederick J. 1969 *Understanding Religious Life*. Encino, CA: Dickenson Publishing Co., Inc.

Stryker, Roy Emerson and Nancy Wood 1973 *In This Proud Land: America 1935–1943 as seen in the FSA Photographs*. NY: Galahad Books.

Swearer, Donald K. 1981 *Buddhism and Society in Southeast Asia*. Chambersburg, PA: Anima Books.

———. 1982 "The Kataragama and Kandy Äsạla Perahäras: Juxtaposing Religious Elements in Śrī Lankā," *Religious Festivals in South India and Śrī Lankā*. Guy R. Welbon and Glenn E. Yocum, eds., New Delhi: Manohar Publishers, pp. 295–311.

Tambiah, S. J. 1968 "Magical Power of Words," *Man*, 2(3):175–208.

———. 1970 *Buddhism and the Spirit Cults in North-East Thailand*. Cambridge: Cambridge University Press.

———. 1986 *Ethnic Fratricide and the Dismantling of Democracy*. Chicago: University of Chicago Press.

Tart, Charles T. 1975 *States of Consciousness*. NY: E. P. Dutton.

Thomas, E. J. 1927 *The Life of the Buddha as Legend and History*. London: Routledge and Kegan Paul.

Trungpa, Chogyam 1975 *Visual Dharma: The Buddhist Art of Tibet*. Berkeley, CA: Rinpoche Shambhala.

Turner, Victor 1969 *The Ritual Process*. NY: Routledge.

———. 1977 "Process, System, and Symbol: A New Anthropological Syntheis," *Daedalus*, 106(3):61–80.

———. 1982 *From Ritual to Theatre: The Human Seriousness of Play*. New York: PAJ Publications.

UN Population Studies (96) 1986 *World Population Prospects: Estimates and Projections as Assessed in 1984*.

van Cuylenberg, Reg 1962 *Image of an Island: A Portrait of Ceylon*. NY: Orion Press.

van der Leeuw, Gerardus 1938 *Religion in Essence and Manifestation: A Study in Phenomenology.* Trans. by J. E. Turner. NY: Macmillan Co. (reprinted 1986, Princeton University Press).

Vansina, Jan 1965 *Oral Tradition: A Study in Historical Methodology.* London: Routledge and Kegan Paul.

von Schroeder, Ulrich 1992 *The Golden Age of Sculpture in Śrī Lankā: Masterpieces of Buddhist and Hindu Bronzes from Museums in Śrī Lankā.* Association Française d'Action Artistque. Hong Kong: Visual Dharma Publications Ltd.

Wachissara, Ven. Koṭagama 1961 *Vālita Śaraṇaṅkara and the Revival of Buddhism in Ceylon.* Ph.D. dissertation *ms.*, University of London.

Wallace, A. F. C. 1970 *Culture and Personality.* NY: Random House.

Walsh, Roger 1977 "Initial Meditative Experiences: Part I," *The Journal of Transpersonal Psychology*, 9(2):151–192.

Wang, Gungwu, ed. 1975 *Self and Biography: Essays on the Individual and Society in Asia.* Australian Academy of Humanities. Sydney: Sydney University Press. .

Watson, Lawrence 1976 "Understanding a Life History as a Subjective Document: Hermeneutical and Phenomenological Perspective," *Ethos*, 4:95–131.

Watzlawick, Paul, John Weakland, and Richard Fisch 1974 *Change: Principles of Problem Formation and Problem Resolution.* NY: W. W. Norton.

Waxler, N. E. 1977 "Is Mental Illness Cured in Traditional Societies? A Theoretical Analysis," *Culture, Medicine and Psychiatry*, 1:233–254.

——. 1979 "Is Outcome for Schizophrenia Better in Non-industrial Societies? The Case of Śrī Lankā," *Journal of Nervous and Mental Disease*, 167:144–158.

Weber, Max 1967 *The Religion of India.* NY: The Free Press.

Welwood, John 1977 "On Psychological Space," *The Journal of Transpersonal Psychology*, 2:97–118.

Wendt, Lionel 1950 *Ceylon.* London: Lincoln-Prager Publishers Ltd.

Wickramasinghe, Martin 1972 *Buddhism and Art.* Colombo: M. D. Gunasena.

Wijayaratna, Mohan 1990 *Buddhist Monastic Life according to the Texts of the Theravāda Tradition.* Trans. from French edition 1983 by Claude Grangier and Steven Collins. NY: Cambridge University Press.

Wijesekera, Nandadeva 1984 *Heritage of Śrī Lankā*. Colombo: The Times of Ceylon.

Wikramagamage, Chandra 1991 *Galvihāra, Polonnaruva: A Rare Creation by Human Hand*. Mattegodagama, Polgasovita, Śrī Lankā: Academy of Śrī Lankan Culture.

Williams, Thomas R. 1975 *Psychological Anthropology*. Chicago: Aldine.

Winslow, Donald J. 1980 *Life-Writing: Glossary of Terms in Biography, Autobiography, and Related Forms*. Honolulu: The University Press of Hawaii.

Wirz, Paul 1954 *Exorcism and the Art of Healing in Ceylon*. Leiden: E. J. Brill.

——. 1972 *Kataragama: The Holiest Place in Ceylon*. Colombo: Lake House.

Worth, Sol and John Adair 1975 *Through Navajo Eyes: An Exploration in Film Communication and Anthropology*. Bloomington: Indiana University Press (original 1972).

Wray, Elizabeth, Clare Rosenfield, and Dorothy Bailey 1972 *Ten Lives of the Buddha: Siamese Temple Paintings and Jātaka Tales*. NY: Weatherhill.

Wright, Basil and John Grierson 1934 *Song of Ceylon*. A film distributed by MOMA and Cont/McG-H.

Yalman, Nur 1962 "Ascetic Monks of Ceylon," *Ethnology*, 1:315–328.

——. 1964 "The Structure of Sinhalese Healing Rituals," E. B. Harper, ed., *Religion in South Asia*. Seattle: University of Washington Press, pp. 115–150.

——. 1967 *Under the Bo Tree: Studies in Caste, Kinship, and Marriage in the Interior of Ceylon*. Berkeley, CA: UC Press.

Yinger, J. M. 1957 *Religion, Society, and the Individual*. NY: Macmillan.

Yoo, Yushin 1976 *Books on Buddhism: An Annotated Subject Guide*. Metuchen, NJ: Scarecrow Press.

Young, Allan A. 1978 "Mode of Production of Medical Knowledge," *Medical Anthropology: Cross-Cultural Studies in Health and Illness*, 2(2):97–122.

Subject Index

account, life 43–47; visual 63–69; *loku hāmuduruvō* 83–92; *basnāyaka nilamē* 101–109; *gurunnānse* 121–129

aesthetics, Sinhalese (grammar of art, composition, *rasa*, Buddhist arts) 18–20, 49, 53–57, 134; choices 54, 75; Arts Council of Ceylon 126–127; symbolized 134

ahiṃsā (non-violence) 13, 102

Amarapura Nikāya (Sinhalese Buddhist sect from Burma established after the Siyam Nikāya, against exclusive castism restrictions) 85

ānācakka (domestic and political order, temporal authority) 78

ancient cities 29

Arts Council of Ceylon 126–127

Ārya (upper Hindu castes) 32

Äsaḷa, Esala (July–August season for festival at temples and *dēvāles*) 94–95, 96, 140, 145

Aśoka (emperor of South Asia during the 3rd Century B.C.) 12, 39, 50–51

asurā, pl. (supernatural beings of great ferocity) 93

āyurveda (traditional Sinhalese medical practice) 143

balanced livelihood (*samajīvikatā*) 75

basnāyaka nilamē (chief official of a Sinhalese *dēvāle*) 7, 17, 18, 75, 91, 123, 125, 140, 142, 145; def. 96–97; life account 101–109

beravā (drummers caste) 121, 123

bhakti (personal devotion to a deity) 94

bhāvanā (meditation) 139, 144

bhikkhu (mendicant, Buddhist monk, a renouncer retaining specific ascetic vows), def. 79–80; *arañña-vāsī* 39; *grāma-vāsī* 39, 90; *tāpasa bhikkhu* (wandering monk) 136

bō-tree 20, 89, 90

British Empire, Colonial 29; administration 40; record 97; tea estate worker 105; army 105–106

buddhāgama (Buddhism) 77

budu gē (Buddha image house) 77, 90